Aboriginal Voices

PAJ Books

Bonnie Marranca and Gautam Dasgupta,
Series Editors

Aboriginal Voices

Amerindian, Inuit, and Sami Theater

Edited by Per Brask
and William Morgan

The Johns Hopkins University Press
Baltimore and London

Inquiries concerning all amateur and professional performance rights
should be addressed to the publisher.

The Johns Hopkins University Press
701 West 40th Street
Baltimore, Maryland 21211-2190
The Johns Hopkins Press Ltd., London

Library of Congress Cataloging-in-Publication Data

Aboriginal voices : Amerindian, Inuit, and Sami theater / edited by
  Per Brask and William Morgan.
     p.   cm.—(PAJ books)
  ISBN 0-8018-4376-6
  1. Theater—Arctic regions—History—20th century.   2. Indigenous
peoples—Arctic regions.   3. Indian drama—History and criticism.
4. Lapp drama—History and criticism.   5. Inuit drama—History
and criticism.   6. Lapps—Drama.   7. Eskimos—Drama.   I. Brask,
Per K., 1952– .   II. Morgan, William, 1940– .   III. Series.
PN2219.3.A26   1992
792'.089'97—dc20   91-44790

Contents

Acknowledgments

The editors would like to thank the Research Committee of the University of Winnipeg for awarding to this project a Social Sciences and Humanities Research Council Research Furlough for travel and a Discretionary Grant for typing expenses.

Introduction

William Morgan

The past ten to fifteen years have seen the rise in many parts of the world of indigenous peoples' theater companies. The terms *aboriginal* and *native* are often applied to performance groups constituted in the main by individuals whose cultural background stems from a group long resident in a locality or region presently under the dominance of a more recently intrusive colonizing group. Theater companies have sprung from tribal groups in colonial Africa, from aborigine tribes in colonized Australia, and from aboriginal groups throughout the whole of Latin America. Mexican-American (Chicano) theater has become well established in those areas of the United States expropriated from Mexico within the past century and more. All of these cultural groups exist under circumstances of some degree of oppression by the dominant society thrust upon them. It would be a facile explanation that attributed the rise of these theater groups solely to a need for the kind of diversion and entertainment that staged performances can and do provide. Something much closer to the bone is at work here, something that has been seized upon by desperate disempowered peoples as a way to heal psychic wounds, communal and individual, and to present their dilemma for consideration to the members of dominant, colonizing societies unaware for the most part of the character of the traditional cultures of those peoples.

A theatrical performance is capable, through dialogue and action, of conveying not only linear but metaphorical information and knowledge. As Richard Schechner has noted: "In oral [traditional] cultures especially, a performance is an art, an entertainment, a ritual, an education, a political manifesto, a social corrective, a repository of folklore, history, and culture" (*Between Theatre and Anthropology* [Philadelphia: University of Pennsylvania Press, 1985], 259).

The editors of this volume have noted elsewhere at considerable length (William Morgan and Per Brask, "Towards a Conceptual Understanding of the Transformation from Ritual to Theatre," *Anthropologica* 30 [1988]: 175–202) that there is much overlap in the functions of communal ritual in traditional cultures and of theatrical performance, which seems to have evolved in the context of the rise of state-level societies. There is an advantage to theatrical over ritual performance for the needs of disempowered aboriginal cultural groups. The scripted dialogue of theater has a high innovation potential with respect to the structure and content of the performance. Innovative dialogue is a rich medium for reactive commentary upon the status quo of the social order under which any given aboriginal group exists. In contrast to traditional ritual, which is fully comprehensible only to the culturally initiated, theatrical performance (dialogue and body kinesics) can select eclectically elements from aboriginal culture along with elements from Western world culture and integrate them into a performance that will touch the sensibility of both aboriginal and nonaboriginal audiences. A piece of aboriginal theater so constructed looks inward and outward at the same time.

Aboriginal groups resident in the arctic and subarctic regions of North America and of Europe have long experienced great disruption of their traditional cultures by dominant, colonizing societies. Alaskan and Canadian Inuit, Canadian and American native Indian peoples, the Sami (Lapplanders) of northern Scandinavia and Russia—all have formed theater groups to tell the stories of their cultures, yesterday and today, to themselves and to non-natives. The scope and purpose of this volume is an examination of the character and the raison d'être of these northern theater groups. To this end, we have solicited from a native dramatist, from nonnative dramaturgs intimately involved in northern indigenous theater, and from an anthropologist essays on topics central to an appreciation of northern performance groups. These essays form the first section of the book.

Three play scripts comprise the second section. The first of these, "Inuit," is based upon myths of the Greenland Inuit (many of whom have

Danish ancestry as well) and upon old Norse myths. This play is the hallmark of the Tŭkak' Theater, which is housed on the rural northwest coast of Denmark. The second script, "The Homecoming," derives from the myth and the contemporary experiences of Alaskan Inuit and originates with the Chevak Tanqik Theater of Alaska. The final script, "Gesat," has to do with the search for, or restoration of, the cultural identity of the indigenous Sami (Lapp) people of northern Scandinavia.

The third and final section of the book comprises a series of interviews with playwrights and dramaturgs, each with a fervent involvement in the creation and presentation of native theatrical performances in northern regions. These guided interviews have an open-ended quality to them that allowed the person interviewed to introduce subject matter that she or he believed to be appropriate and of importance. Whereas each interview has its expected idiosyncratic character, it is nonetheless instructive to note the commonalities of interest and opinion among those interviewed.

The essays, the scripts, and the interviews all resolve into several topics concerning the purpose and character of northern theater. Many worthy theater groups and dramatists receive no mention in these pages due solely to considerations of book length.

Empowerment of Indigenous Groups

Joshua Weiser's essay "Indigenous Theater: A Path toward Cultural Empowerment" is most explicit in informing the reader that a major mission of the Chevak Alaskan Inuit theater is to provide communication skills to performers and a solid sense of cultural identity to the people of Chevak. A consequent elevation of self-confidence increases the likelihood that their voices will be clearly and strongly heard by dominant, non-native Alaskan society.

Edith Turner's essay on recently revived North Slope Alaskan Inupiat Inuit ritual performances makes apparent that these revivals do not evoke nostalgia in Inuit participants and Inuit audiences. Rather, they constitute a claim on their heritage, a taking back of something lost for decades, a way of closing ranks to deal from a strengthened position with pressures from non-Inuit society.

Jordan Wheeler, writing about aboriginal "voice," indicates that aboriginal theater and literature must serve as a means of communication of native solidarity across the plurality of native Canadian cultures to strengthen native identity, dispel the ethnocentric depiction of native cultures held by Euro-Canadians, and combat the racism that has relegated native people in Canada to a historical footnote in the development of the nation.

Using Theater as a Healing Process

A theme encountered repeatedly throughout the following essays, plays, and interviews is that of native theater arts as a powerful healing tool. The artist—the playwright, the performer—is a healer; he or she does not teach directly, but opens the way to insights that aid in the healing of native individuals and communities that have suffered often severe trauma at the hands of the colonizers.

Tomson Highway, Cree playwright, tells us in an interview that years of intimate contact with native people on urban Canadian streets compelled him to begin writing plays incorporating native myths, plays to act at once as a balm and a clarion call to the sensibility of native audiences.

The Danish dramaturg Kirsten Thonsgaard presents the reader with an essay on the effects upon her own psyche of her long-term association with the Tûkak' Theater. This theater was established in 1975 at a time of cultural and political upheaval in Greenland, four years before Greenland home rule. The performances mounted by this company (see the "Inuit" script to follow) constitute a search for cultural identity on the part of native Greenlanders. As Thonsgaard entered into the performances of Tûkak', she gradually experienced the removal of a feeling of oppression hanging over her head, something long since created by "academic and ideological fatigue." The plays of Tûkak' were not linear, problem-resolution productions, but were based on elements of Inuit and Norse myth, creating a sense of life force and metaphoric insight into the human condition. Many members of the Tûkak' company responded in a similar manner to their experiences in that group.

Reidar Nilsson, artistic director of Tûkak' Theater, tells us in his interview how he began that theater after seeing the powerful and beneficial effect that a small performance of a Greenland Inuit myth had on native Greenlanders. The potential of theater to heal an injured cultural identity was made clear to him.

Jordan Wheeler, in the essay "Voice," has this to say about healing, whether through theater or literature: "During five hundred years of contact, the lives of aboriginal people have borne an onslaught of pain and tragedy. The result is a beleaguered, traumatized people suffering deep wounds. At present, the aboriginal community is healing, and stories that reflect the struggle, and the resulting harmonious existence within a given environment, help the healing process."

Aboriginal and European-style Theater

Edith Turner's essay "Style and the Double Mind in Inupiat Eskimo Traditional Performance" deals with the revival of several pre-contact rituals among these Inuit groups. She sees the ancient traditional kinetic action and song as working on the secular level of spectacle, entertainment, but in addition and more fundamentally on a level of consciousness where the spirit nature of existence is evoked. Traditional performance and song, over and above any text or dialogue, characterize aboriginal theater and evoke in native audiences (and, to an unpredictable extent, in non-native audiences) a sense of contact with an extra-ordinary realm of being. Turner even states: "I am tempted to ask whether present-day experimental theater has to be "sanitized" in some way against the effects of performing ritual-like acts. Or are there unavoidable natural consequences in Order Two [spirit nature of existence] to a bodily performance whether one is aware of it or not?—a disturbing question."

The Inupiat rituals are communal, multicommunity in fact, and not meant for non-Inuit observers. This is not theatrical performance, but it foreshadows it. The major ritual subject of this essay, "The Messenger Feast," was held in an elementary school gymnasium at Point Barrow, with the gym bleachers and the stage giving something of a theatrical effect to the proceedings. Television cameras recorded the event. Even now dance troupes such as that of Point Hope "exist in a world of public performance such as art events and what are basically political meetings such as the Alaska Federation of Natives." Clearly there are no unilinear social evolutionary processes at work here where, by the addition of dialogue and such elements, an Inupiat aboriginal theater would unavoidably emerge. The preconditions for such an event are present, however. The Inupiat case represents a situation that might give rise to aboriginal theater.

The Danish playwright Ulla Ryum has had personal contact with the culture of the Sami people for over thirty years and has assisted in the establishment of Sami theater, the Beaivváš Theater in Kautokeino in particular. She notes that the Sami have a proclivity to express things in non-Aristotelian ways, in visual terms rather than verbally. However, she taught the Sami Aristotelian forms of story construction as one kind of performance tool. Ryum notes that Sami theater began organizationally on a Western model of authoritative, hierarchical structure and control, but that kind of structure soon dissolved in favor of an organizational form more consistent with the egalitarian, cooperative structure of traditional Sami society.

Reidar Nilsson based the development of the Tūkak' Greenland Inuit theater on the proposition that theater can work only if it is artistically sound. Actors are trained as such, not as Inuit or Sami actors. The play "Inuit" is not a traditional piece, but a contemporary amalgam of elements of Greenlandic and Norse myth, with a use of dialogue and staging familiar to Western theatergoers. Although "Inuit" represents a search for cultural identity, the structure of the piece is not one of problem and linear resolution on an Aristotelian model. It is not political theater that tells people how to think and live. The play deals with the way in which the White Spirit (cultural imperialism) has forced masks onto the Inuit people. Using the resources of spiritual strength of traditional Inuit culture, each individual must struggle within him- or herself to become whole again. Greenlanders are deeply touched by these insights, the significance of which has not been lost on the non-Inuit audiences in those many European and North American locations where "Inuit" has been presented.

The Chevak Alaskan Inuit Theater under the guidance of Joshua Weiser and John Pingayak has developed scripts based on Inuit myth (always validated by village elders) and the contemporary situation in the Chevak region. Traditional myth, dance, and song are incorporated in a textual Western-style stage presentation with one salient feature of traditional ritual: those attendant participate in the performance, with "plants" in the audience inciting it to move the action forward in less than predictable ways. The piece "Homecoming" exemplifies this.

Alan Filewod's essay on how non-natives watch native theater contains a warning about the importance of physical setting for the successful presentation of aboriginal theater. A piece presented by the Tunooniq Theater, an Inuit theater group from Baffin Island, "appropriates certain elements of Anglo theatrical performance into the cultural field of the Inuit community." The play, when presented in the Arctic to Inuit people, in a community hall or open-air space, relies heavily for the transmission of its meaning upon the context or matrix of its performance. When Filewod saw the play on stage in southern Ontario, there was "a cultural transformation that erased much of the meaning of the performance. . . . The performance ran the risk of turning itself into a costume drama . . .

the drumming, traditional clothing, dance steps" were the basis of the performance. In the final analysis, the play does successfully articulate cultural conflict to Inuit and non-Inuit audiences alike.

Knut Walle and Kurt Hermansen of the Sami Beaivváš Theater view the mission of the theater as the strengthening of Sami cultural identity. They defend the introduction of Western theater into a culture without a theatrical tradition by saying that it is up to the indigenous culture to choose which aspects of world theater are incorporated into its performances, and to integrate these elements with traditional performance. In communicating Sami culture through theater, visual imagery is very important, as many Sami do not understand their ancestral language and no European language is a suitable vehicle. Visual imagery, always central in ritual performance of indigenous peoples, takes on an added dimension of importance with respect to the mission of all aboriginal theaters that find themselves in a similar linguistic dilemma.

Tomson Highway attributes the unique quality of native theater to the body of native myth (Cree and Ojibway in his case) from which the scripts are drawn. Unlike the Western world view, Algonkian cosmology does not admonish, does not treat of the triumph of good over evil (or the reverse) in a linear plot line. Insights are metaphoric, casting light, if not resolution, on the human condition.

Authenticity

The myth, the song, the dance that impart so much of the structure and content of aboriginal theater: How do we know they are authentic? Who would ask this question, and what is meant by it? It seems largely to be a question of concern to "purists" with a static conception of traditional culture as something ancient, fixed, immutable. Richard Schechner has said, "Modern sensibility wants to bring into the postmodern world 'authentic cultural items.' Maybe this is just a kind of post-imperialist souvenir hunt. Or maybe it is something more and better" (*Between Theatre and Anthropology*, 114).

Edith Turner asks whether the revised Inuit rituals she witnessed on the Alaskan North Slope are authentic. Her answer is yes, they are. Any changes in those rituals from sixty or eighty years ago have been implemented by Inupiaq in order to better meet the requirements of ritual under their current circumstances. Cultures and their ritual performances always change, sometimes very slowly, sometimes quickly, but always "authentically."

The "Inuit" script, hallmark of the Tükak' Theater, is a fusion of Greenland Inuit and Norse myth, staged in a Western world manner. Is the content of "Inuit" authentic? It is so because just that admixture of cultural elements, Inuit and Danish, characterizes Greenlandic culture today and has done so for some considerable time past. An authentic Greenlander identity must draw from these cultural roots.

Kirsten Thonsgaard indicates in her essay that, during times of unrest in Greenland prior to 1979 Home Rule, there was a tendency to distinguish between "authentic" Greenlandic values (in everyday life as well as theater) and those that were "pseudo-Danish." The resolution of this debate came through Greenlandic voices that pointed out that such chauvinistic attitudes were in fact very much contrary to old Greenlandic values. The Tükak' Theater represented accommodation.

Play scripts for the Alaskan Inuit Chevak Theater are written by Joshua Weiser and John Pingayak. The authenticity of fact and of voice is always checked out with village elders and a wider cross section of the community. The works' authenticity in terms of tradition and the contemporary situation of Chevak is judged by the people who are subjects of the scripts.

Tomson Highway views the authenticity of a native theatrical performance in terms of faithfulness to the character of the aboriginal myths upon which the play is based. The Cree and Ojibway Trickster figure (so important in the Highway interview) can function fully as well and authentically in downtown Toronto as in Brochet, Manitoba.

Voice

When a work of theater or of literature treats of aboriginal culture, but when the information, the message transmitted, does not come from the perspective of the world view of that culture, and when the presentation is based on misconceptions of aboriginal culture entrenched in the works of non-native historians, academics, and fiction writers—then the work does not have an "indigenous voice."

Jordan Wheeler's essay, "Voice," speaks for a myriad of native playwrights, fiction writers, and native persons aware that only if the voice is true to native values and cosmology can theater and fiction heal within and set aright mistaken non-native conceptions of native cultures. Wheeler makes a convincing case that it must be aboriginal people who write about aboriginal cultures (specific cultures, not "generic aboriginal"). Will non-natives continue to write plays and novels about native cultures? Yes, they will, but it is important that such writers exercise integrity, be as accurate as possible, work with native people in the production of the work. Even then, Wheeler sees a serious problem with non-natives' speaking as if with aboriginal voice.

Richard Schechner has addressed the problem of native voice, of non-natives writing about natives. He sees the danger here as the "imposition of alien categories on Third World [sic] cultures" (*Between Theatre and Anthropology*, 309).

In the same way that Euro-American Joshua Weiser works with Inuit John Pingayak, along with village elders, to ensure Inuit voice is present, Knut Walle of the Beaivváš Theater works closely with producer Kurt Hermansen, a Sami, to produce theater pieces with authentic Sami voice. The Sami play "Gesat" (see Part II) was written by Walle collaboratively with the Sami actor and film maker Nils Gaup (also known for his film *The Pathfinder*, which received a Best Foreign Film Oscar Nomination), whose voice is that of the "acculturated" Sami artist solidifying the cultural identity of the Sami people.

Tomson Highway speaks in his interview of his perception of the need for institutions that will provide a vehicle for the voice of native playwrights and actors. The establishment of Native Earth Performing Arts is one successful attempt to meet that need.

Alan Filewod's intriguing essay "Averting the Colonizing Gaze: Notes on Watching Native Theater" bears directly upon the notion of "native voice," not with respect to its utterance but to its apprehension by non-native viewers of aboriginal theater. He sees the Anglo response to indigenous theater performance as "sincere but problematic." To Anglos there is the danger of receiving such a performance as "a quaint depiction of the folk life of a marginalized community . . . a jolly celebration of an eccentric culture."

Filewod reminds us of the fact that the more authentic the native voice in a theater piece, the less readily accessible it is to non-native audiences. Describing his experience of a Tunooniq Theater (Canadian Inuit) play, Filewod notes that the basis of the play is not in language, not in speech, but in gesture "and the gestures are those of a culture for which I have almost no reference"; nor does he have the basic critical language to describe such a performance. Turner, Thonsgaard, and Nilsson suggest in their contributions that there may well be a degree of universal understanding, metaphoric though it may be, of certain elements of the language of gesture. Certainly Filewod was moved by the Tunooniq performance and seemingly moved in the direction intended by the performers.

Multiplicity or Monoculture?

"Many people these days fear a disruption of historical cultural variety brought about by world monoculture. Just as physical well-being [of a biological population] depends on a varied gene pool, so social well-being depends on a varied 'culture pool' " (Schechner, p. 114). Ulla Ryum asks that one be accepting of the multiplicity of cultures, of the variety of world views that exist. Celebration of the richness and uniqueness of one culture must not bar anyone from learning things of value from other cultural perspectives. Indigenous theater is admirably suited to this learning task.

The essays, play scripts, and interviews that follow speak directly to the need of colonizing societies to hear the voice of the indigenous peoples they have long dominated and never truly cared to understand in their own terms. The voice of native peoples is strengthening; the lot of aboriginals as a "sidebar to history" is no longer bearable. The ancient pain of their oppression and the newly emerging joy of fellowship in the renewal of unique cultural identities are palpable to any of us who will learn to listen with respect to another's story, and to watch as unfamiliar gestures on stage evoke in us an awareness of the many-named life forces that envelop us all.

I
Essays

Style and the Double Mind in Inupiat Eskimo Traditional Performance

Edith Turner

Recently there have been revivals of pre-contact rituals on the North Slope of Alaska. This was a surprise to me, the researcher on the spot, for I had been sunk in the everyday world of the modern Christianized Inupiat on the North Slope studying Eskimo healing, and had settled in my mind that nothing could be revived. Authentic African ritual was surviving, as I have reported in *Performing Arts Journal* ("Zambia's Kankanga Dances: The Changing Life of Ritual," *PAJ* 30, 1987), but I had given up hope of Eskimo ritual apart from the whaling festival. Now, as the revivals arose, I began to perceive in them and in the so-called secular dancing an expression of a kind of double mind consisting of the everyday secular mode, which I shall call Order One, and the released or climactic, Order Two. The two showed different forms of consciousness, the latter appearing to spring from what the Eskimos know as the spirit nature of existence. The release has to be invited, conjured by hesitant steps—a process seen in the soft and loud stanzas of the songs and in many episodes of the Messenger Feast, which was the principal˚ of the revived rituals I am discussing.

The Inupiat Eskimos are hunters. They contrive to catch whales for their food, seeking these fifty-foot monsters in sixteen-foot skin boats, knowing the uncertainty of the enterprise, and understanding from their personal experience the need for a collective spirit for its success, and also the need for connectedness not only with each other but in a mystical way with the animal itself. The performances of these people speak strongly of such a level of relationship. But the level is not easily won. The forms of performance tell the story of that difficult approach more clearly than words can do. In this essay I attempt merely to give a picture of the performances, hinting (which is the Eskimo way, not the Western way) where we encounter the signs of the other level, the other mind, the double of the ordinary much as Artaud identified it.

Charlie Kinneaveauk was showing me the Kaviatchaq dance of the First Full Moon. I was in his house at Point Hope in a snow storm; it was March 1989. Charlie put on a simple mask made of whale baleen, with walrus ivory eyes and two snowy owl's feathers stuck out in opposite diagonals above his head.

"We have a puppet, this big." He indicated a length of about eighteen inches. "It goes along the ceiling, see, on those strings, and halfway along is what we have here, something like a seal bladder blown up." He showed a large styrofoam ball. "The puppet needs six strings and twelve men to work it properly. The puppet is an Eskimo person. We made it out of baleen and some thin wood from kerosene boxes. It has its legs jointed with rubber. See, it starts dancing like this."

He leaned over wearing the mask. He did nothing for a while. Then he twitched his right foot. He twitched an arm; then his head and both arms, then he jerked his head and whole trunk at an angle to the right, then suddenly to the left, glaring out at nothing with a surprised grin. A comic. (Long ago the anthropologist Froelich Rainey, in *The Whale Hunters of Tigara*, [New York: Anthropological Papers of the American Museum of Natural History, 1947], 250, described this "slow-getting-quicker" dance.) Normally men would be drumming and singing in the brisk syncopated beat of Eskimo music.

Now on the other wall appeared an animal, a marmot—it must have nosed out of a hole in the wall. It was quiescent on the strings. As Charlie sang and manipulated strings it jerked a little forward. Then a little again. It came across in tiny syncopated movements to the rhythm, passing the bladder, arriving at the opposite wall, and then its furry body contorted strangely and it doubled back on itself to take the return journey. Its legs hung down moving with the motion; the legs bore no paws, consisting merely of hanging fur which moved. Its real animal nose led it onward, and behind hung a real tail. When it turned again I had cold chills.

The person-puppet was ready. It hung quiescent, then it twitched its right foot. Slowly it began the jerking dance to the music, making its way across, never moving the left foot. Its first angled glance was at the bladder. It went toward it, caught it, dragged it down, and clutched it over its heart, with both its arms crossing. Immediately the music stopped. Then it released the bladder, which went up again.

It is from this slow animation of an inanimate thing that the Eskimo style of dancing derives. It is called "the awakening dance." Also that hesitant alternation of action, Charlie's side-to-side jerking, is another aspect of it, very much related to the coming and going of spirit awareness.

Let us hear the description of an old man who worked with the afore-mentioned Rainey, Tigluk Oviok by name. Tigluk called this event Uku-taaqtaq, the ancient dance.

The curtain is closed before they start. There is a lit candle out in front. The drummers, singers, and actors get ready. One person opens the curtain and announces the event. He does this singing, very slowly and soft, "now they're hunting." When he's done they close the curtain. They open it again and he sits, singing the song of the medicine people. He moves his right foot just a little; and then moves his left arm. Soon he stomps with his right leg in time to the drums, but he never moves the left. A third time they open the curtain and he sings. Then one drummer sits in front and the drummers follow, slow and quiet. The dancer moves his body to the right side as he sings, then moves his body to the left side. He sings of hunting. That brings the animals. When he moves to the right side the drummers and singers go faster. Now the man sits on the floor and tries to blow out the candle by moving backwards without turning around. He does it, and they go on playing in the dark. One man is in front and two on each side; there are two men behind the row of singers at the corners. They wear a headpiece with feathers set at an angle. They peek out just a little bit with their feathers, gradually peeking higher and higher. There are various designs on the seal skin on the front of the headpiece, a walrus, whale, polar bear, beluga whale, goose, seal, and so on. The songs are hunting or emergency songs.

Many dancers, men and women, come out gradually from the right toward the front with their arms linked, each holding up a stick. They circle around and go to the left, all joined together.

We can see in both descriptions the "now-you-see-it-now-you-don't" characteristic: Charlie Kinneaveauk's slow start, then his sudden jerking, peering movement, throwing himself away from the act as it were; and the marmot's disappearing and reappearing, climaxed by the puppet's convulsive hugging of the bladder in which the spirit of the seal rests (vividly stating the identity of man and seal). In Tigluk's account there is the candlelight giving way to darkness, then the "peeking" and gradual emergence and awakening of all the men and women dancers. Both performances, themselves revivals, took place at a revived festival in January 1989, which I learned was the greatest of the lost Eskimo rituals, the Messenger Feast.

Three men, the Eskimo savant Ernest Umigluk Frankson, George Ahmaogak, mayor of the North Slope Borough, and Red Okakok, another Eskimo patriot, were instrumental in reviving the Messenger Feast. The location of the performance was the elementary school gymnasium in Barrow three hundred miles to the northeast. Fifty-two of Point Hope's dancers flew by plane over the icy wastes and frozen sea to get there, answering the "message" sent by "messengers" (actually by satellite telephone) to all the villages to foregather at the Borough center. The gathering was for their own sake this time, no tourist performance this; yet with the gym venue and gym bleachers in full sight creating a stage effect, it was inevitably a performance. Present-giving, that emotional exchange closely related to the potlatch, was a strong part of the revival. Valuables such as skins, furs, meat, guns, radios, stereo sets, and books changed hands. The emotion was expressed in the joint dance of giver and receiver that always followed the rather casual presentation. Way back in the past, the spirit of the eagle, the founder of the Messenger Feast, taught many arts to humankind in the course of teaching this ritual: respect for the animals, the art of drumming, the art of exchange—freely giving one's all—and the art of the messenger staff, on which were tied tags representing the needed goods—the prototype of writing and the checkbook, as Ernest Umigluk put it. The story of the eagle came to my ears piecemeal. The original man to whom the eagle showed these acts was, shockingly, the man who had killed the eagle. However, he behaved respectfully toward its body, taking off its skin with care and setting it to dry. By this means the spirit of the eagle was able to take on its parka—its body—again, and be alive once more.

So some rarely seen rites were performed in the gym that winter. It is not accidental that much was done with strings at this performance, as is fitting for people who invented many string figure games. Catching, tying up, and then magicking to make it come alive is the name of the game. The marmot puppet on strings was performed as Charlie Kinneaveauk described it—and received frowns from the stricter church adherents in the hall because it was "devil-worship"—but delight from the majority.

It would be hard to separate the marmot figure from that of an animal called the kikituq, a shaman's familiar who disappears and reappears out of his master's sleeve, who dies when his master dies and comes alive again, beneficent when well treated but deadly as an enemy, a wonderful help in hunting. The consciousness of animals as potentially beneficent spirits has not left the Eskimos and is not likely to do so, in spite of continuous church opposition in the region.

Along with the marmot dance came a curious divination act, done with a carved object which was in effect a hand-held spinning top. Jacob Lane of Point Hope fashioned a large dome-shaped top out of wood, incorporating a peg which projected below. This peg fitted loosely, with ample room, into a separate hollow handle. Before fitting together the two parts, top and handle, a string was wound many times around the peg and passed through a hole in the side of the handle, and then the top with its peg and string was fitted onto the handle. When Jacob gave a sharp pull on the string emerging from the handle the domed top spun rapidly around. In addition notches were cut in various places on the top and the notches stuffed with duck's down feathers. At the ritual this curious object was taken out and spun, whereupon the feathers flew out, signifying by their abundance or paucity the hunting outlook in the coming whaling season . As with dice or the roulette wheel, the spinning top carries a kind of "will-it-happen-won't-it-happen" character—chance being part and parcel of the spirit world, and the answer given by chance being a message of true divination. But what happened at the ritual in January 1989? Jacob worked the oracle, but he stuffed the holes with damp feathers and they did not fly out. This meant there would be no whales. Sure enough, I later heard by satellite telephone the distressing news that during the whole of the whaling season from March through June the hunters of Point Hope caught not a single whale out of their quota of six. The weather and ice conditions made it impossible.

The enactment in the gymnasium proceeded, fulfilling another serio-comic ritual of ancient times. Men and women lined up in two rows facing each other, with a wide space between. Those in the rows were the guests whom the messengers had invited. Now two bowmen entered between them, feinting and aiming, causing comic terror in the two ranks. Many of the faces had been whitened, "so that they were unrecognizable." Here was much hesitation. The old idea ran like this: was the visiting party friendly or hostile? In ancient times the spirit directed, and took the badly intentioned arrows off over the heads of the guests. Here of course the

The Bow and Arrow Dance

same thing took place, the arrow flew above the heads of those lined up amid delighted laughter. According to early accounts the approach of the band of visitors to the host village was choreographed by many such sensitive ritual events, for example, the presentation of a tiny amount of food, which was the first hint of commensality, and the teasing and mock anger, to try out the strength of good feeling. These were "social" arts, the skills concerned with contact between two stranger groups, not yet the art of simulating the eagle himself, which latter is so closely related to theatre and concerned with what I am calling Order Two, as we shall see. With more general reference to this order, I am tempted to ask whether present-day experimental theatre has to be "sanitized" in some way against the effects of performing ritual-like acts. Or are there unavoidable natural consequences in Order Two to a bodily performance, whether one is aware of it or not?—a disturbing question.

There were two climaxes to the Messenger Feast, the climax of giving, and the coming of the eagle spirit. The gift presentation went on at Barrow all through the dancing, adding presents of fur-lined boots, stereos, a roll of tricolored calfskin, even a drum (worth $450)—valuable and honorable presents that really hurt to give. At the turn of the century a man went totally bankrupt rather than fail his messenger-guest. The qalgi used to be piled to the roof with presents, leaving the recipients overcome with emotion—just as I saw among recipients in Barrow in 1988. This was the Order One climax.

The Order Two climax came immediately. The men brought into the gymnasium a small electric hydraulic lift. One man entered the operator's box and was elevated to the ceiling, where he managed to sling a rope over a girder. Several fascinated children and I watched the machinery but the crowd did not, for such a sight was ordinary enough to these Eskimos. The men proceeded to suspend from the rope a box drum. This was the style of drum given to humankind by the eagle spirit. Around the top of the drum's wooden edges ran wooden zigzags—these were the mountains which you can see inland, the mountains where the eagle's mother had her home and over which the shaman hero flew on the back of the eagle. Up along the side of the box was fixed a sounding rod topped with a snowy owl's feather. The drummer beats this rod, which in turn strikes all along the side of the box drum. The whole drum swung gently on its rope until the men were ready.

A thousand Eskimos seated on the gym basketball bleachers were now breathlessly waiting. The missionaries had banned the Messenger Feast in 1908. Now it was appearing again. TV cameras were set to record; the borough mayor and elders gave their speeches, not a word of which referred to the eagle, for this was a public occasion and it wouldn't do. But the dance was to tell its own story.

Ernie Umigluk warned me to look for the *slow* drum and the *fast* drum. And slowly I began to see the story in the dance, the importance of the kinetic actions. In a row a little behind the box drum and on either side of it sat four dancers, young Eskimos wearing enormous gaily trimmed mittens (their wings), headbands set with feathers, and traditional mukluk boots. These men sat with their backs to the people; they were bent over, negative, passive. Behind them again sat a row of regular drummers with women singers at their back. In front of the box drum sat the elder drummer waiting, with the drumstick held behind him. Down his back you could see two wings, loon's wings from the loon headdress he was wearing, and in front you could see the loon's beak sticking out from the headdress over his brow with a ball suspended from it. The ball, the "sun," is usually shown in iconography in the Raven's beak, for it was Raven the creator who brought daylight to humankind. Four powerful

The Box Drum

birds are already represented here, snowy owl, eagle, loon, and raven—symbol upon symbol, a surplus of signifiers, to use Barbara Babcock's term. Suddenly, this central figure twitched his drumstick: the four eagle servants behind jerked an inch. No, it was nothing. He twitched again . . . nothing. (It was that slow beginning I was learning about.) He positively swung the drumstick in a arc to make a beat.

The eagles rose slightly and lowered again, for the beat never connected. We do not know how they saw his actions with their backs turned. Then, he struck. The drumstick connected, singing broke out, the eagles rose slowly, turning around as they did so, while the drummer continued beating with a mighty swing at every stroke, grabbing the handle of the drum and rotating the whole drum with ferocious energy. It was the flying. The eagles were already thrusting those immense mittens continually before them. Music poured out from the ranks of drummers and women behind, led by a woman elder who it now appeared had been commanding the whole performance with a stick in each hand. The drummer, old Andrew Ekak, the grandfather of my neighbor's children, swung and beat

The Eagle

and swung and beat. The eagles kept their left feet firm while stomping with the right, with their bodies bent over and arms thrusting down continually. As Tigluk said, "All the singers and drummers look down, they look down"—and here Tigluk bent low. "They never look up until the curtain goes down."

The drummer suddenly wrenched the box violently to the left and beat a compelling drumroll upon it. The eagles all turned to the right, away from him, and fluttered their wings to the right. He wrenched the drum to the right and beat a roll. The eagles bent and fluttered toward the left and stayed there, their hands twitching to the stick's command. Ekak pointed his drumstick right across his body and far down toward the floor to the left. All the eagles bent low at this signal and crossed their wings before them. The drummer struck the drum and feinted again to the left. They crossed their wings again and trembled, and again whenever he beat the drum and thrust the stick down to the left. Then suddenly from behind the drummer came forth another figure, waving its arms up and down as it danced forward this way and that. It stayed violently jackknifing right behind Ekak. The crowd roared because they knew the meaning of what was going to happen (and this I did not realize until years afterward). The new figure was the spirit of the eagle seeking rebirth. It snatched the loon cap from Ekak. Ekak immediately helped him put it on. The figure snatched Ekak's drumstick and replaced him as the drummer of the box. Ekak left the scene flying with jackknifing arms. *He* was now the re-fleshed eagle. The dance continued in its frenzy with the new drummer swinging and beating away as hard as he could. As for us, we were flying to the mountains on the eagle's back, on Ekak; we were in the realm of shamanism.

None of these spirits were mentioned in the Eskimo magazines and press. Only Ernie Umigluk, whose great-grandfather Umigluk was gifted with Shamanism and gave personal power songs (as they put it literally) to his village, would talk about it, and then tentatively, fearing trouble.

Finally, the "awakening," "pulling," "going out," "being born" (ani-iraq) dance began with the men and women dancers edging out in a line from the right behind the drummers, little by little. They made their way forward making a wide semicircle around toward the left, at each fourth step pausing to dance for several moments on the spot. Each dancer stretched out her right arm behind her, holding upright in her hand a baton tipped with a snowy owl's feather. She kept her elbow bent sideways in the direction she was going, moving over sideways, pushing as it were the dancer at that side who was also moving sideways, whose own feather-tipped baton was reaching back almost to touch her, "pulling" her along. So they all progressed in a slowly dancing chain, rhythmically linked by elbow and feather, stopping and starting again with synchronized bending steps. The sound, "kii," arose, "let's *go*," in a low unison roar as they urged still further forward, until all had emerged, slowly, often pausing like the marmot, and completed the half circle around the drums. I commented to Ernest Umigluk, "There is so much hesitating, stopping, and starting. . . ." He said, "Isn't that appropriate? Wouldn't you?"

"Yes," I said. It is hard to be born, to go outside; but tradition has a secret. It says that just as you leave that place, which in the old days contained the feathered skin of the eagle hanging over a beam, you would hear heartbeats coming out of the skin, loud, then fading into the distance as the eagle's new spirit-body flew far over the mountains back to its mother. Those heartbeats were the drum beats and the drum beats were the heartbeats.

For eighty years Eskimo dancing has been performed without ritual because dance was officially secularized. However, its nature inevitably consisted of Order One and Order Two in the way I have described, which is something germane to the dance itself. Let us look at its nature, its style. Regular Eskimo dancing is performed to the sound of large tambourine-shaped drums nearly two feet across with narrow rims provided with a handle, and stretched with a skin made from the lining of a walrus's stomach. The skin has a great capacity to give out a booming sound. However, the drum is never beaten on the skin but on the far side of the wooden rim and from beneath, using a long flexible drumstick. A long whack on the rim will cause the skin to boom simultaneously with the sharp clack of wood on wood. It is this mixed sound that excites.

A party of drummers, familiar with each other's company, strolls into place and each seats himself on the ground with a water bottle to wet the skin. Women line up behind. One or two words pass between the company and the drums start moving lightly up and down, with the men softly swishing the sticks to merely touch the opposite rim from below. It is a sort of breathing time. They sing, but the voices are tentative and soft. Out in front stand a man and a woman, their arms barely moving, the man's right foot tapping occasionally. Suddenly the sound changes. The same song comes out in force. The women's voices resemble the harsh sound of wood, high and immediate. The drums' clack-boom jumps into heady rhythm, a steady yet somehow syncopated beat that almost makes you choke with its unexpected gaps and starts. "Yaa-yaa-yaa-yaa!" go the voices, sonorous, gripping the rhythm in compulsive squeezes, no pretty hymn tune this. And at the end, where are we? Quite lost, because the stanza ends unexpectedly, on the supertonic. The Eskimos look at one another secretly in enjoyment. Meanwhile the dancing has been going on in force.

The couple stands apart, the woman with her feet immobile and her knees flexing to the beat. Her head nods, her body nods, her arms describe—like calligraphy—certain extraordinarily complicated arabesques, here, there, up, wide, beckoning, sighting, drawing, all in the

The Eskimo Stomp

compelling rhythm. It is a simple beautifying of the way of life, a reflexive act that transmutes that way into Order Two—crystallizing it out into angles and facets and perfect numbers. The men seem to be leaping, but that left foot does not leave the ground. It is a kind of leaping stomp, exciting in its implications of possibilities not realized. The arms fly around in the same complex motions, bird motions, with the head at curious angles, poking and dissociated. Ernie said that a dancer *looks* at nothing, though his face glares in all directions. Here indeed is Order Two. This dancing "brings the caribou."

The dancers quarrel. Two factions in the village dispute the honor of being first. One elder abuses another publicly, and the abused one, a very honored man whose scholarship in the field of language is said to be the work of a miracle, suddenly tears off his dancing tunic and throws it on the ground. Terrible gossip arises from this incident. It is nothing but the conflict that arises from the limited good, for the Eskimo-Indian Olympic authorities would not allow Point Hope's very large dance troupe to compete; its size would make the judging unfair. The troupe was forced to divide, causing internal competition in the village. These dancers exist in a world of public performances such as arts events and what are basically political meetings such as the Alaska Federation of Natives. Thus we find "secular" dancing, which passes over so often into Order Two dancing, dynamizing the tribal gatherings.

Let us watch this old Eskimo scholar teaching his troupe something he is trying to remember. They are seated in a row in the Kalgi Community Center, a geodesic dome built by a Minnesotan architect. The old man is in the middle of the row, younger ones on either side of him. There is silence. He merely seems to be nodding to himself. He lifts his drum a fraction, taps. Silence. He starts a very quiet song to himself, tapping like a whisper on the drum. Next time through he is singing it. The others are still quiet. He repeats. And then their drums raise, they tap too, and you hear their voices. The song quickens; this one can't have been sung for sixty years. All have it now, and they belt it out—it is like discovering the Lost Ark, this is no nostalgia, it is a *claim,* it is grabbing back what is theirs.

I am trying to put over what it is in the Eskimo dancing style. This soft/loud, this hesitation/breakthrough, this slow start is an approach method, a divination method, aimed toward something that hatches out, breaks out of a protective membrane. Simply, the soft stanza in the common dance with the strong stanza following is the prototype of this. What you break through to can even bring the caribou; it is no small thing. In the pre-contact days of shamanism, of course, the drumming of the shaman made an explosive breakthrough (well described for a drummer of another race by Maya Deren, who experienced Voodoo). The Eskimo breakthrough felled the shaman to the floor and his spirit left its body to travel far under the ice. The slow working up to pressure that we see today was also a feature of a certain old ritual faculty, something that used to be called "shaman tricks" by the whites. A shaman locked into his sod house walked three times around the room, then flew up to the skylight and escaped. Another shaman caught on an ice floe gently drifted to land and he was able to walk off. There is a "going inside oneself," according to well-proven custom; then the release which propels the performer into Order Two.

There exists the further question of authenticity. Was the performance I saw this competitive songfest in a school gymnasium really the Old Messenger Feast? Among people who watch cable TV continually, how can whaling and the old values survive? This is a question that has much troubled white sympathizers. White friends, including me, attempt political moves. The Eskimos welcome help, but their shoulders are literally and metaphorically stronger than ours. *They* have decided to revive their Messenger Feast in this particular way; revivals often do not please the purist, but it is *their* way, their self-determination governing what should take place. To be truly non-imperialistic we have to accept that way, not a better way we might think up for them. The very ritual ideas change, so that there is no one way.

I have often thought about the whole mess of politics as it relates to the predicament of the native peoples of the United States and the Inupiat in particular. Do we regard the revival of the Messenger Feast as a political statement? Is its cultural value secondary to its function of bonding an oppressed group together, and preserving morale until the Eskimos can regain their proper position in this land of extraordinary greedy whites, avid for sport hunting, avid for "the unspoiled places"? We all know how attractive those places are. (Who is without fault?)

What is the Eskimos' proper role in the world of today? To trade whale meat for an income, when the whale is sacred? (They would not use the word *sacred,* they are too modest, but they know the animal as a spiritual being that should be respected.) Or should we see to it that the Eskimos are preserved in their traditional ways and become enclosed in a pod of living history? Somehow that isn't fair. The fact is they are doing their own organizing well enough. What is required is for the whites to cease whittling down their rights. Looking at the Messenger Feast in the school gymnasium we see it as a sign of the inner regrowth of the people themselves. They are revealing again something of their enacted religion, which is more than a morale raiser (though the organizers did hope it would combat alcoholism), more than a political statement. It is what it is: for them it is the eagle at work, an animal which like the whale never dies, but returns in a new parka again and again.

Note: I am using material collected on trips to the Arctic from August 1987 to August 1988 and for short periods in 1989 and 1990. My thanks are due to my sponsors, the Wenner-Gren Foundation for Anthropological Research and the University of Virginia. The help given by James and Mary McConnell is warmly acknowledged. I am particularly grateful to my consultants and coanalysts, Ernest Umigluk Frankson, Tigluk Oviok, Jacob Lane, Charlie Kinneeveauk, Loretta Kenton, Susie Frankson, Chris Wooley, Rex and Leona Okakok, Bill Hess, Molly Oktollik, and many friends in Point Hope, also Lori Courtney-Krumm, Karlene Leeper, Ann Fienup-Riordan and others from outside who instructed me or made my way easier. I am grateful for the photographs of the Kirgiq Messenger Feast, which were taken by Bill Hess.

Edith Turner is a lecturer in the Department of Anthropology at the University of Virginia, Charlottesville.

Averting
the Colonizing Gaze
Notes on Watching
Native Theater

Alan Filewod

I can't write about native theater; all I can write about is my response to it. When I watch native theater I see my own gaze returned; my watching is an appropriation, even when it is invited. As the colonizer I am the invisible presence in these plays.

The plays I'm talking about are part of the current renaissance of native Indian theater in Canada. Despite our official myth of multiculturalism, for the most part Canadian theaters still verify the white/patriarchal power structure of our society. In the theater that structure has been challenged by the historically disenfranchised communities: women, gays, and cultural minorities have begun the long process of transforming our notions of what theater is and our aesthetic responses to them.

Native Indians have long been the most severely oppressed of the minorities in Canada. Here, like the rest of the Americas, the native peoples are living through times of rapid historical change. But land claims settlements and more rectifying legislation have not rolled back centuries of vicious racism and genocide. At the same time it is the native artists who are most visibly challenging the Anglo-patriarchal assumptions on which our theater is built.

My greatest difficulty in expressing my thoughts on the recent development of this native theater arises out of the absence of a critical vocabulary that articulates the contradictions of colonialism. Even the language of difference comprises semiotic constructs that reduce the complexities of colonialism to a relatively simple problem of ethnicity. The formulation of a critical response requires that I speak of native culture in opposition to what is usually called "Anglo" culture. I must begin then by defining the field of these labels. "Anglo" is used here not to denote ethnicity but as a code to signal the dominant culture of the colonizer, the culture of which I am a part, and as a critic and editor, a perpetuator. Although my culture and its notions of theater have silenced minority voices, the dialectic of that colonialism is complex, because the theater attracts many who have other experiences of oppression, and whose working lives as marginalized artists constitute another form of oppression. The colonized person defines the self in terms derived from the colonizing power while at the same time seeking definition in resistance. The historical experience of the Anglo-Canadian artist is one of defining the self as a colonized subject, colonized by the cultural hegemony of the United States, colonized by the social formation that devalues the work of the artist, colonized by patriarchy and sexism. Having defined myself in these terms for years, it is not easy to admit my role as a colonizer in the Anglo/native dialectic. To be an Anglo-Canadian artist is to live with a destabilized notion of the self.

If, for the moment, *Anglo* denotes the colonizing culture that oppresses native Indian culture, *native* is here used to denote the colonized culture of the many native Indian and Inuit nations in Canada, and is not meant to eradicate differences between those nations and between the various community and legal conditions under which they live.

Ask anyone who is up-to-date on Canadian theater who the hottest playwright in Canada is, and you will invariably hear the same answer: Tomson Highway. Born on a Cree reserve in northern Manitoba, trained as a concert pianist and composer, now artistic director of Native Earth Theatre Company in Toronto, Canada's foremost professional theater run by native Indians, Tomson Highway's arrival as Canada's playwright-of-the-moment is based on a small canon. His reputation in fact rests mainly on two plays, *The Rez Sisters* and *Dry Lips Oughta Move to Kapuskasing*. Linked by a common setting and a strong web of intertextual references, these plays are set on an Indian reserve on Manitoulin Island in northern Ontario. (Native Earth is closely related to De-Ba-Jeh-Mu-Jig Theatre on Manitoulin Island, where *The Rez Sisters* was workshopped in 1986, but it reaches further to join a network of native theater culture; *The Rez Sisters* also included members of New York's Spiderwoman troupe.)

In *The Rez Sisters* a group of women put aside their differences and travel to Toronto to the world's biggest bingo. In *Dry Lips,* the men of the reserve, some of them married to the women previously met in *The Rez Sisters,* confront their political impotence as the women—first the women of the reserve, then all of the native women in Canada, then all native women in the world—invade the men's domain and take to the ice to form a native women's hockey league.

In both plays comedy of character and community life expands to mythic proportions as a simple metaphor (the bingo game, women on ice) grows and transforms into a satiric gesture that reconstitutes the action, as if a sit-com turns into Aristophanes. The classical reference isn't entirely inappropriate, because Highway himself has said that *Dry Lips* is built around the cosmic conflict of Hera's furious jealousy over Zeus's infidelities.

The agent of the transformation in both plays is Nanabush (the Ojibway name for the Trickster, known as Weesageechjak in Cree and familiar in English as Coyote). Nanabush, in Highway's own words, "can assume any guise he chooses. Essentially a comic, clownish sort of character, his role is to teach us about the nature and the meaning of existence on the planet Earth; he straddles the consciousness of man and that of God, the Great Spirit" (Highway 1988, p. xii). Because the Ojibway and Cree languages that permeate the plays do not differentiate gender, Nanabush is both male and female.

Nanabush's polysexuality is crucial to Highway's political statement, because both plays demonstrate that the emancipation of the native peoples proceeds from the empowerment of women. In the most horrifying episode in *Dry Lips,* a mute young man, damaged by his delivery from a drunken mother on a bar-room floor while the men stood and watched, rapes a woman (who is herself an incarnation of Nanabush) with a crucifix. The men live in fear of women's sexuality, which is figured in the play by the immense breasts, belly, and bum that the actress playing Nanabush dons to distinguish the several women in the play. We are always aware in both plays that Highway is a male engaged in a subversion of this own male construction of the female.

Highway's dramaturgical struggle is to reclaim cultural power by reviving mythic structures that have been erased by colonialism. The struggle is made complex by the fundamental problem that a colonized people is brought up within and as part of the cultural formation of the colonizer. The posture of the native artist is one of internalized contradiction; in their thematic and dramaturgical structures Highway's plays manifest a double vision that incorporates the colonized self and the colonizing other.

Highway's plays manifest that duality through Nanabush, the trickster who is at once an agent of randomness and at the same time an orchestrated dramatic element. This is why Highway's plays can be so difficult for the urban audience. The dramatic form is predicated on a Aristotelian causality but is given the semblance of randomness. In *The Rez Sisters* and *Dry Lips* the action turns on Nanabush's interventions, but these sequences are difficult to follow because the Trickster's character and powers are never made clear to the audience. Nanabush's presence is literally mystifying; the transformations that he/she imposes on the action originate in a non-European logic system that by definition cannot be wholly explicable to the colonizer. The confusion I register when watching Nanabush at work replicates the confusion Nanabush brings to human affairs within the play.

How can the language of drama, a causality derived from the colonizing power, and which establishes an inviolable structuring of action, contain within itself the randomness that Nanabush represents? Highway's solution is to juxtapose familiar dramatic causality with the inexplicable actions of the Trickster, whose motives and purposes remain ambiguous. Nanabush shows us that all is not as simple as it seems, that beyond the familiar actions of daily life there is another plane of meaning that we can only glimpse. Nanabush is never articulated as a character as such, but as a refracted image that intervenes in the action. He/she is given material form in a series of disguises; in *The Rez Sisters* Nanabush (represented by a male dancer) appears as a seagull, a nighthawk, and the Bingo Master; in *Dry Lips* he/she appears as the spirit of the three women whose sexuality defines the male community. Through Nanabush, Highway subverts the fundamental laws of dramatic action.

But does he subvert his own subversion and demonstrate an allegiance to the gaze of the colonizer by the romantic ending of *Dry Lips,* which rationalizes the irrational elements of the narrative as a mystical dream? *Dry Lips* builds on two thematic patterns: the first narrates the women's assumption of power through hockey; the second brings past and present together in the story of the damaged young man and his violent attempt to reclaim identity through rape. The final image of the play is "a beautiful naked Indian man lifting this naked baby Indian girl up in the air, his wife beside him watching and laughing." Our colonizing gaze establishes an ordering which subordinates the mysticism of the play to the etiology we bring to it. Highway's plays are built around a memory of traditional culture that values family, sexuality, and birth; read from the outside that memory is reduced to a romantic icon of spirituality and invincibility.

This emblem of purity is troublesome because it doesn't translate; it transforms its meaning according to the audiences' relationship to the colonialism that underlies the play. What has happened here? The contradictions of colonialism are recursive; they fold inward on themselves. Consider the levels on which they work. The implied audience of the plays is urban, largely Anglo—products of the colonizing culture formation. The establishment of professional arts awards Highway its highest honors: the Governor General's Award for Drama, a Chalmers award for best new Canadian play; the Wang International award for best new Canadian writer, four Dora Mavor Moore awards for *Dry Lips*. These awards were given not out of something as simple as liberal guilt but out of identification. Highway's peers are genuinely celebrating a new and powerful voice. The response is sincere but problematic.

It is problematic because this celebratory response erases the politics of the play and reestablishes the narrative as a generalized statement of anticolonialism, permitting the colonizer to assume the posture of the colonized. It is inevitable that we should come to Highway's plays though an identification with the oppressed characters rather than an awareness of our place as colonizer, because the historical project of Canadian theater over the past twenty years has been the legitimization of a post-colonial voice that narrates the history of Canadian culture as a struggle against models derived from Britain and the United States. Anglophone Canadians—those of us who have not already surrendered entirely to the colonizing embrace of American mass culture—perceive ourselves as colonized, as bit players on a world stage. We find it more difficult to acknowledge our role as colonizers than Americans do, because Americans have a tradition of liberal dissent against the empire they have built. Our empires are smaller and more local, and we haven't wanted to admit them. Consequently, not only do we erase our own culpability in Highway's plays, but we reconstruct their cultural patterns to serve our own cultural project—a project that has historically erased the native peoples.

Recently I spoke to an urbane British critic who had seen *The Rez Sisters* at the Edinburgh Festival. He said to me, "It's all right but it's really just a community play, isn't it?" To him, the play was a quaint depiction of the folk life of a marginalized community. I suspect that is how many of the urban Toronto audience receive the play: as a jolly celebration of an eccentric culture peopled with larger-than-life characters blessed with funny names like Emily Dictionary and Philomena Moose-tail, who happen to be, because of their rural existence and Indian culture, "more authentic"—meaning more sexual, defined more by their appetites and spirituality—than we are.

The latest development in recursive colonialism is that *Dry Lips* has been picked up by a major commercial producer. What will the play say to the commercial audience? It is in any manifestation a statement of empowerment, but in the context of commercial production, the voice that initially empowered a minority that struggles daily against poverty and racism now empowers the colonizing majority with a more comfortable message that native culture still survives, is growing stronger, that the problems we read about in the newspapers are working themselves out on the community level. The anger in the play—the anger of the people whose colonized existence turns them against themselves, the anger of native men who begin to understand that power resides in the women—is transformed through a change in material conditions and audience into sentimentality. Put simply, it lets the Anglo audience off the hook. If it didn't, it could scarcely appeal to a commercial producer.

The trap is to construct the dialectic in the reductive terms of "progres-siveness." Certainly it is progress when a native playwright redefines the terms of Canadian drama; certainly it is progress when a commercial producer pours money into a Canadian play rather than the usual Broadway and West End hits. But with equal validity it is regression when that redefinition upholds the cultural myths by which Anglo Canada excuses its marginalization of native Indians.

My fear is that so long as Highway narrates the native struggles as a process of spiritual regeneration audiences will be less accepting of an angrier voice that narrates the struggle in terms of political action. There are native theaters that define issues in more political terms, but they have been largely ignored by the Anglo cultural establishment (whose response they may not seek). A case in point is Monique Mojica, whose *Princess Pocahontas and the Blue Spots* (also produced by Native Earth) is a feminist condemnation of racist male exploitation of native women. Do we applaud Highway's plays because we can write into them the image of the native that makes us most comfortable? If so, what choice does Highway have? It is not my place to offer a solution to him; mine is part of the critical voice that wants to embrace his work in the theoretical field of Canadian drama. My gaze colonizes; it cannot be averted. And I cannot make Highway responsible for my own contradictions.

Native Earth is redefining native Indian drama, within the native community and within the Anglo cultural mind, that much is obvious. But the challenges it presents are not being recognized by the theatrical community; instead we have rushed to embrace the work of this company without critical discourse or self-analysis. When critics rave about Highway's work they translate it into a self-congratulatory discourse: See how sophisticated I am; I appreciate this work. See how *multicultural* we are; we honor this work. See how (and this is the recurring theme of Canadian critical discourse still) *distinct* (that is, non-American) we are; we are part of the community generated by this work.

But we aren't part of that community, not without abdicating our responsibility to confront our own roles as colonizers. That is perhaps the most difficult posture for the Anglo-Canadian, which is why we are such effective and such insidious colonizers. Wounded Knee was south of the border, right? We've made historic land claims settlements, right? And because we never did adopt Jeffersonian democracy in Canada, we can always pass the buck to "the government" (symbolized not by the people, but by the now purely emblematic and almost forgotten fiction of "the Crown").

Native Earth reaps honors, in part because it is situated in Toronto, where this is the only native theater the critics see, partly because Highway is by any reckoning a powerful and innovative writer, but also because we are comfortable with the message we hear. But Native Earth is not the only native theater in Canada. Probably no one can say how many there actually are, because most of them operate sporadically on short-term grants. But there are two others that I have seen recently that would never have a chance in hell of attracting a commercial producer. My experience of these companies leads me to question our mis/reading of the political aesthetics of Highway's work.

The first of these groups in Tunooniq, an Inuit company operating out of Pond Inlet on Baffin Island in Canada's Arctic. Tunooniq visited Ontario last year when it played in Guelph at the Bread and Butter festival sponsored by the Canadian Popular Theatre Alliance. Although Guelph is only fifteen miles from Toronto, and the visit was well publicized, Tonooniq's first-ever appearance in Ontario failed to attract attention— let alone attendance—from the audience that celebrate Native Earth.

Tunooniq's work appropriates certain elements of Anglo theatrical performance into the cultural field of the Inuit community. Consequently, it is so specific to its origins that it is difficult for us to "read" it out of context. Instead of a community hall or outdoor playing space, I saw them in a theater, on a stage—a cultural transformation that erased much of the meaning of the performance. Nevertheless, what I saw held me in awe in a way that Highway's plays do not.

That night in Guelph, Tunooniq performed two short pieces with four actors: two Inuit women, one Inuit man, and an Anglo woman. The idiom of the performance was dance and mime. In the first piece, a shaman reminded the community of the power of the rapidly eroding traditional values of the community. In the second piece, another shamanistic figure helped a young woman struggle against the bonds—literally figured as a webbing of ribbon—of drug abuse. In both cases the living presence of historical social values was articulated through traditional dance, drumming, and invocation.

On the stage in southern Ontario, the performance ran the risk of turning itself into a costume drama, because the very elements that ground the performance to its implied audience were those that underlined its exotic difference to us. To the Inuit audience (I assume), the drumming, the traditional clothing, the dance steps were the basis of the performance; our southern gaze identified the icons of realism in the elements alien to traditional culture, like the young woman's heavy metal t-shirt. To both audiences, however, the play articulated a conflict between cultures registered in the semiotics of performance.

Where the experience differed most vividly from my experience of Native Earth was in the reading of the acting itself. Of all the fields of difference in the theater, acting style and technique are the most complex, because acting is conceived in terms of a "naturalism" that remains culturally specific and undefined. One of Native Earth's greatest contributions has been the development of native Indian actors who no longer have to conceal their origins in order to find work. Its commitment to native performers means that Native Earth cannot always rely on professionally "trained" actors. The company redefines what we expect from an actor. Why should we demand perfect diction, concert-hall projection, Broadway "crispness" from actors to whose performance culture these values may not be pertinent?

The acting in Native Earth challenges and redefines our prevailing notions of acting in the professional theater. The important point here is that it is an acting style that can be comprehended within that notion; it is informed by the same models of performance that underlie most approaches to acting in Canada. The acting in Tunooniq is different, and I'm not sure we have the vocabulary to describe it. It is not based in language and speech but in gesture, and the gestures are those of a culture for which I have almost no references. David Quamaniq is one of the most impressive performers I have ever seen, but I don't have the basic critical language to describe his performance. All I can do, all any colonizing gaze can do, is see the difference. This is the ongoing paradox of the colonized, who are always constructed by the colonizer as the other, recognized mainly by the degree of difference from the self—a difference that the colonized, as a strategy of protection, attempts to reduce. In this case, the difference that held me most vividly was the amount of joyful *play* in the performance, as the narration would periodically segue into brief routines of Inuit dance games that seemed to be included mainly for the sheer fun of it.

The difference in response is easily explained, of course. Tunooniq lives and works in a community that is geographically and culturally far away from mine, although the very subjects of the performance suggest the distance is not as great as we might like to think. But the actors of Native Earth work and live in Toronto; they participate in the larger field of professional theater in the city. The difference in performance is not as easily recognized. It was most apparent when *The Rez Sisters* first performed in the Native Community Centre on Spadina Avenue; it was less apparent when the show moved to the Factory Theatre. But the factory is a small space, and we were close enough that the performances could still overcome the colonizing formality of the theater. What will happen when *Dry Lips* is remounted in the Edwardian splendor of the cavernous Royal Alexandra Theatre? My guess is that the embrace of the colonizer will almost completely eradicate that difference.

Native Earth tries to integrate this colonizing gaze by situating itself in the world of the Anglo audience. Tunooniq performs almost exclusively for its own community. This suggests a typology of native theater polarized by the implied and actual audience. If that is the case, there is a third model situated between these two, represented by Headlines Theatre in Vancouver.

Unlike Tunooniq and Native Earth, Headlines is an Anglo Theater company, which is to say that the company is mainly administered and directed by non-natives. Headlines is what is known in Canada as a "popular theater"; it works with community organizations to create advocacy theater on a variety of social issues. Headlines's work with the Gitksan and Wet'suwet'en people of northern British Columbia led to the evolution of a performance called *No' Xyra'* (Our Footprints), which tribal elders approved as a vehicle to disseminate their point of view in a difficult land-claims case that has been dragging through the courts for some years. The play developed through workshops in the community, and was performed by a mixed cast of native and Anglo actors. The playwright and director, David Diamond, is a non-native. Each performance was validated by the community through the presence of a representative of the tribal elders, who accompanied the show on its national and New Zealand tours.

No' Xya' offers a different take on the representation of the colonized figure. It narrates the history of the Gitksan and Wet'suwet'en nations as one of struggle to hold on to sacred land. The narration draws upon traditional performance motifs; the play begins with Guu Hadix, the spirit of the salmon, telling the history of the people:

> The Gitksan and the Wet'suwet'en peoples are made up of many Clans which include Fireweed, Beaver, Frog, Wolf and Eagle. They live in a territory that covers 22,000 square miles. (*rattle*) They are bordered on all sides by different nations. The Nisga'a, Tsimsian, Haisla, Tahltan, Noo'tsinii, Chilcotin, and Sekani. (*rattle*) The first Chiefs of the Gitksan and the Wet'suwet'en walk the land and become one with the spirits and life forms there. (*rattle*) They place their canes in the earth—merging the power of the land, the animals and themselves—creating a bond of respect with all life that will never be broken. (*rattle*) In this way they mark off their territories as their own.

The narration is supported by nonverbal action derived from traditional dance, using authentic regalia, and songs passed on from community elders. The manuscript of the play is extensively footnoted: every story, anecdote, song, and quotation as well as factual information is attributed to the source person who provided it. In some instances that information is privileged; this is the case with one sacred song that the company was given permission to sing in the performance but could not include in the written text.

This attribution, which marks the company's allegiance to the cultural priorities of the community, justifies the representation of native images by Anglo actors, and validates the opening presence of Guu Hadix as an authentic voice of power. The voice of the colonizer subordinates itself to the voice of the colonized?

Is it possible for the colonizer to surrender power? In this case the performance text continuously authenticates its representation of the colonized. This is done mainly by the fact that the representation is controlled by native structure of cultural authority, and by the dramaturgical framework. The central issue of the play is that of ancestral land, which we see during the course of the action appropriated and transformed by the Anglo settlers. The two Anglo actors portray generations of settlers; the two native actors portray the parallel generations of the displaced. The contradictions of colonialism, which change according to historical conditions, are sketched through this series of brief confrontations, contained within the governing narration of Guu Hadix. The ideological statement of the play is articulated in the very fact of the performance, so that the narrated conclusion, that it is just that Anglos surrender privilege to rectify historical crimes, is a restatement of the very premise of the performance, a premise the company attempts to incorporate into its actual working process.

Through its analysis of historical crime, *No' Xya'* postulates a postcolonial community in which the Anglo colonizer surrenders to the older power of the colonized native. This is predicated on the acceptance of the native religious statement that sacred power resides in the land, and touches all who live on the land. This is a more radical statement than is to be found in Highway's work, where Nanabush is clearly identified as a part of the native soul which cannot be eradicated or appropriated by the colonizer. The statement here is even more radical because it is made by an Anglo theater, which brings it perilously close to the kind of romantic appropriation of native culture that has historically excused genocide. In this case, the subordination to the hereditary chiefs of the Gitksan and Wet'suet'en legitimizes the embrace of native religion. The suggestion of metaphysics is made within the field of politics, and the final statement of the performance resolves the development contradictions of culture, religion, and colonialism by turning them back to the authority of the colonized:

> As is also the tradition in the Feast Hall, we would like to ask you, our honoured guests, to speak. To share your truth and understanding about ancestral land and self-government with us. We have Ardythe Wilson here tonight who is representing the Gitksan and Wet'suwet'en Hereditary Chiefs to respond to any questions you might have. We are going to take a short break first so you can stretch and gather your thoughts. Before we break, we would like to thank our sponsors for this evening. (*He/she does*)

Oh. For those of you who got trees—please, take them home, put them in the fridge and plant them tomorrow, OK? Thank you and please come back so we can talk.

When I watch Tomson Highway's plays I am discomfited by the unresolved relationships of colonialism; my gaze is returned but my power as colonizer is unchallenged; ultimately I am afraid that my response disqualifies itself. When I watch Tunooniq I am enthralled by the presence of a traditional culture that mine is erasing, and I grieve for the damage we have done; I wonder how the Inuit will resolve this contradiction we have forced on them. When I received a tree at the end of *No' Xya'* I felt privileged; the tree was a gift and the gift demanded reciprocation in the form of political support. *No' Xya'* shows the way to true post-colonialism; it shows that the only way the colonizer can achieve empowerment is by surrendering power.

Alan Filewod teaches drama at the University of Guelph, Ontario. He is the editor of *Canadian Theatre Review*.

The Spirit of the Tũkak'

Kirsten Thonsgaard

I grew up in a tiny house in a small settlement. There was quiet. Time. Time for people to exist in quiet with themselves.

I remember a beautiful summer day when everything was shining and it was very quiet. I was six or seven years old. I looked out of the window and I experienced the power of this quietness. It dug itself into my very being. But, outside, on the horizon I suddenly saw something ugly approaching. It was grey and pale. I could sense it before I knew what it was—I think that at that time we were still part of a process whereby you could connect with that which is called "the air" (Sila). You could sense when there was something not right in your environment—the change in the air. The damnation which descended on us. We were told that our settlement was going to be closed down. I still see it sharply in my mind. We were all Greenlanders, sealers and whalers, in the settlement; we'd never seen any Danes.

My father . . . No, I don't want to talk about that! . . . It was so humiliating.

I often feel as if I'm standing between two different kinds of air. Moving from one to the other. Moving back and forth. That's not good. My air becomes unclean. I become depressed. I start to rot inside. I begin to lose my soul. And, I'm unable to find help anywhere. But, then the human being inside of me awakes and says stop. I call for help. If my cry is strong enough and sincere enough the spirits will come to my rescue.

29

But, if your cry is not sincere and rooted in your very being, well, then
the spirits turn against you.

Bendo Schmidt, January 25, 1979

It was a winter's day; the sun was shining and the frozen snow
cracked. Jutland's west coast in Denmark. The name of the village is
Fjaltring. The Tûkak' Theater is located there and had been there since
1976. It occupies an old, renovated farm right next to the North Sea. I
spoke to Benedikte Schmidt (Bendo) in the workshop while she was
working on a mask. She was one of the actors who had been with the
Tûkak' since its founding in 1975. She had participated in the "birth" of
the show "Inuit," which was and still is the theater's calling card. She
had performed in the show in Alaska, Italy, Canada, and during the first
extensive tour of Greenland in the summer of 1978. She had participated
in spreading Tûkak's name around the world.

So much had happened. So much success. It was wonderful—and
charged with responsibility. So many thoughts to struggle with. Hope for
the future, for Greenland—1979 was, after all, the year of home rule—
and for Bendo herself. Because the plan was that she would complete her
formal training at the Tûkak' Theater the following spring, and after that
she would return to Greenland—perhaps together with some of the others,
Rassi Thygesen, Moses Aronsen, Naja Qeqe, Soré Møller, and Rasmus
Lyberth—to start the theater or the theaters Tûkak' had cleared the path
for. That had been the idea behind the whole thing.

Now she sat across from me, the mask in her hands. She told me about
her thoughts and about her life. We tried to get to the very core of what
it means to be an actor—and a woman and a Greenlander. What did the
working methods of the Tûkak' mean to her? How was it to be a member
of the company at the Tûkak' Theater? I had interviewed her, and the other
actors, several times during the previous couple of years. I'd attempted to
get to the heart of what made the Tûkak' Theater such a completely unique
theater. A place for actors who prepare, who are being trained, who create
art—in order to create life. We talked about the past and about the future.
We also talked about politics.

The 1970s was an era of ideologies. The spirit of the time was characterized by unrest, showdowns, confrontation, and the expectation of political
change. In Greenland political parties with clear ideological stances had
arisen. The tone of the debate had hardened. Difficult and challenging
issues were being discussed. Issues that were of concern to every Green-

lander, such as the discussion about "Greenlandic identity." Could you call yourself a Greenlander if you didn't speak Greenlandic? If there were Danes in the family? If you thought "in Danish" but looked like a Greenlander?

In Denmark interest in Greenland and her conditions had ignited again, as it had every few years since the Second World War. But whereas this interest during the sixties had been expressed in "humanistic" terms, it was now directed toward an understanding of political and economic conditions. Danish left-wing intellectuals conducted Marxist analyses of Denmark's "imperialist exploitation of Greenland." Analyses which the new left wing in Greenland adopted and used in its argumentation for Greenland's independence from Denmark.

There was at the time a tendency to cast an interpretation of art and culture in political terms. There was a kind of pride in the old culture and a desire to preserve it and exhibit it, from a new angle. This cultural "awakening" and search for Greenlandic "roots" did not avoid the ideological lopsidedness which often occurs when a people is fighting for independence. There was a certain propensity to distinguish sharply between "authentic" Greenlandic values and those that were considered "pseudo-Danish," imported. But moderate Greenlandic voices were also heard in this debate, pointing out that when "pride" at being a Greenlander turns into chauvinism then it becomes an un-Greenlandic trait!

In the middle of this time of unrest and upheaval the Tūkak' Theater was founded in Denmark. I first heard about the Tūkak' in Greenland in 1976. This was my first encounter with Greenland. I was there to teach a course in drama at the School for Social Pedagogy in Nuuk. I'd arrived with some extremely simplistic and academic ideas about what was going on in Greenland. I wanted so much to show "solidarity" with the Greenlanders! But the reality of Greenland hit me like a torpedo. The ground was pulled from under my feet. I started to see everything from a different perspective. Greenland was so beautiful and so unpredictable. Her nature was so powerful. And Nuuk was pretty and so peaceful—despite its bad name in Denmark. And the people? As different from one another as everywhere else, of course. I met so many with beautiful spirits: easily provoked to laughter, friendly, with a wealth of psychological resources, and talented.

Actually, I felt paralyzed. I found it awkward standing there as a Danish drama teacher. It was painful to assume the role of the "expert," being unable to speak Greenlandic and unable really to understand anything! How was I to touch the emotions of these people through drama? From where did I get the right to?

I thought about the raven in the story about "the soul of the whale and its burning heart." The curious raven that picks at the heart. Should I just pretend I didn't notice and play the role of the raven? No!

Later on I realized that I had over-reacted. It was typical that my scruples were all-important to me. They probably didn't mean much to the Greenlandic students! They were, after all, used to all sorts of Danes. Both the arrogant kind who treated them as culturally "underprivileged" as well as we brooding doubters who were nothing but one big excuse for ourselves. They must have found me comical! That happens when you strain yourself so much—and people haven't the foggiest what's hurting you so badly! But something had "burst" inside of me. I just didn't know what. I tended to interpret things in an ideological manner. After all, I had myself experienced that it was not Danes who should get Greenlanders involved in drama. The Greenlanders had to do that by themselves. And so it was my brain that led me to the Tūkak'. As well as my senses and my emotions.

When, after a long trip by train and by bus I got off at a gravel road far out in the country and started to walk up toward the Tūkak' Theater, there was only the ocean, the sky, the smell of late summer coming from the fields—and an immense stillness—enveloping me. I entered the house, met Reidar Nilsson and his wife Elin, and I felt I'd been welcomed.

The relationship I entered into with the Tūkak' achieved its form. It was rational and useful. I applied for and received a grant in support of a research project at the University of Aarhus, "On the Tūkak' Theater and Its Effect on the Development of Greenland's Cultural Politics during the Years of the Introduction of Home Rule." In the following years I published articles, I met with Greenlandic and Danish politicians, and contributed in this way to an increased interest in the Tūkak'. Yes, I was probably useful—and I was happy about that.

But now so many years later I see clearly what was the real importance of my contact with the Tūkak'. It affected my life. It changed me. It removed a heavy, awkward weight which was encircling my head. It removed a weight that had been created by academic and ideological fatigue and by my distance from creative and life-giving forces. Is that so strange? Not for anyone who has ever experienced a Tūkak' performance. I've spoken with many who have. People of completely different backgrounds, Danes and Greenlanders. They all experience their encounter with the Tūkak' as an incredibly important part of their lives—something which they'd been ready to receive without realizing it beforehand.

If "science" and "love" can be said to be separate kinds of air, I think I ended up being "unscientific!" Otherwise this is a false configuration, because, of course, one can research subjects which become part of oneself and of which one becomes a part. The real problem is rather that one tends to become frightened by one's own level of engagement and responds by busily attempting to remain on the outside. But, once through this phase, one discovers that critical thinking does not have to exclude love. If you want and if you dare you will get closer to the core of the process itself, where everything is as yet unformed and in a state of movement. If you don't dare, if you are afraid to be "subjective," you will ask questions from the periphery.

In the beginning of my relationship with the Tūkak' I experienced time after time that Reidar Nilsson would resist or laugh when I asked "peripheral" questions. Whenever I used terms like "political conscious-ness," "social stratification," and "target group," he would answer me with terms like "the creative forces," "the tree of life," and "the individual human being"!

I recall an episode that touched me deeply. I was eager to do well and I had sent Reidar a draft of a newspaper article about the Tūkak'. I was going to submit it to a paper which had become notable at that time for its critical analyses of "the Greenland question." I'd written the article in a supercilious academic manner—an attempt to please the intelligentsia! Reidar became furious. He asked, "What do you want? "Do you want to be ideological and academic, or do you want to create life?" I was mortally shocked but I grabbed hold of the chance his anger offered me. Fumbling, I tried to tell him how I really felt and what I really wanted. It was the first and last time I had such a clash with Reidar. But now I realize how wonderful it was that he met me in anger—rather than with indifference.

To be honest toward one's own innermost being. Not to hide behind facades. To dare to give oneself fully in the work. Not to rely on other people for the supervision of tasks—or to execute them. To be present here and now. To accept your circumstances, the good and the bad, and to stop all the explanations and excuses for your life. To work toward a goal which is unknown and for which no word exists. To desire to create life! That was the spirit of the Tūkak'.

Everyone who came into contact with the theater felt it, including some of the young Greenlanders who came to train as actors at the Tūkak' but who gave up. Many of them were talented but they could not cope with the peculiarly unlimited freedom of this place combined with its extraordinary demands on each individual. It was so different from other educational institutions in Denmark, where they were used to being greeted with "consideration" and "understanding" because they were Greenlanders! Reidar refused from the very beginning to function as a "social services officer" or as a "babysitter" for the Greenlandic students. He knew well that he could be seen as being hard and "inhuman." But if the Tūkak' didn't effect the same high demands as any other acting school it would be Utopian to believe that these Greenlandic acting students would be able to complete their education and meet the demands of working later on in Greenland as actors, artistic directors, and animators.

It was difficult. Not a single one of these young Greenlanders had lived a harmonious and uncomplicated life. They had faced early separation from their families, social problems, cultural and linguistic displacement. There was so much sorrow and hopelessness. To be involved in the Tūkak' was the most beautiful thing that had ever happened to them. This was the only place where they had been greeted with love. And still it didn't work out for several of them. Especially I remember one of the students. He cried from happiness at being at the Tūkak'. But he disappeared. I saw him several months later. He was staggering about in the train station of a small town, drunk out of his mind. He smiled when he saw me— then he cried. Quietly and for a long time. But now he wanted to go home to Greenland.

"Back home to Greenland"—and back to Denmark. This unending pendulum in the soul. Its movement could be felt in the young actors at the Tūkak'. The restlessness, the feeling of rootlessness . . . and still, to be at the Tūkak'. A third home. Not Greenland, but also not the kind of Denmark they knew from earlier. Geographically it was removed from the culture of the big city with its noise and diversions. It was a small place by the big ocean. Though not a monastery dedicated to inward contemplation, it was a place with a life and an atmosphere all of its own.

Many visitors came through. They'd have to travel to get there. I have often thought about how the landscape and nature assisted in clearing one's mind. When total darkness descended on a winter's evening, when the wind cut through your clothes taking your breath away, and when the ocean thundered earsplittingly close-by, it felt like a reminder, albeit in an unthreatening form, of how perishable a human being is. When you arrived out of breath and wide awake, tore open the door to the Tūkak'

Theater to be received with warmth, light, and laughter, well, then you'd had the peculiar experience of realizing how much human contact really means. To be expected and respected as a guest. No matter who you were. Greenlander or Dane. The minister of culture or a local fisherman. You were simply a person.

I am well aware that I seem to be painting an idealized picture. A dream. But why is it that we don't believe that dreams can come true? Whether it was through "the spirit of the air," Sila, or some other spirit, the Tūkak' had been endowed with a "soul" and a "spirit." Artistic inspiration, spiritual and physical energy filled up the rooms and took possession of us—and we felt a deep sigh and began to breathe calmly.

The legend of "The Holy Gift of the Feast" was the Tūkak's starting point back in 1975. They dramatized the legend and performed it at the Greenlander house in Holstebro. This legend followed them through the years. In 1979 it turned into a new show, *Nattoralik*. But on a different plane Tūkak' realized the legend every day—in their productions, in their way of working, in their way of being together. There are even those who have called the Tūkak' Theater "The Eagle": the one who gives inspiration and teaches. The habitat of the eagle is the air, the spirit, but with a connection to the earth and roots. In Nordic mythology the eagle sits at the top of "the tree of life," Yggdrasill, which shoots deep roots down into the nether world to the wellsprings of life. But in Nordic mythology the serpent, Nidhug, is gnawing at the roots, threatening life. In the legend of "The Holy Gift of the Feast" death and annihilation are likewise the preconditions for the feast and joy. Only when the humans realize that death is inevitable do they begin to understand life. They are shocked out of the "living death" they existed in before. Afraid, they hold on to their only child. Reluctantly, they let him go. Hesitantly, they receive him when he returns with "the holy gift of the feast." And finally they give in to life and joy.

There are dark forces in life and in each individual. Without a connection to these one can't be human. Without confronting these powers in oneself, without exploring them and giving expression to them one cannot become an actor. Life and light arise from the dark. The Tūkak's special form of spirituality is informed by this insight. The longer you live the truer these things become. The Tūkak' is in my soul.

But, imagine, the Tūkak' is not just a frame of mind! That what's so great. Since its beginnings the Tūkak' has worked nonstop. They have created productions, performed innumerable shows, begun cultural initiatives, offered courses, given birth to new ideas, trained actors, participated in conferences and projects, struggled to survive economically, submitted tons of applications, spoken with many, many people all over the world, made an impact on the living, moving world.

What joy!

(Translated from the Danish by Per Brask.)

Kirsten Thonsgaard is a dramaturg at the Aalborg Theater, Denmark.

Voice

Jordan Wheeler

On June 23, 1990, when the Meech Lake Accord officially died on the floor of the Manitoba legislature and Canada as a nation remained incomplete, one man stood before a media scrum and spoke to the world. Like no other aboriginal person before him in the history of aboriginal/Canadian relations, Elijah Harper had voice, and therefore aboriginal people had voice.

On July 11, when five hundred Sûreté du Québec launched an attack on a Mohawk barricade on the First Nation of Kahnesatake, a seventy-eight-day armed stand-off developed between Mohawk warriors and the Sûreté du Québec and the Canadian army. Across the country aboriginal people reacted and the local populations heard it. There was an aboriginal presence, but it was not voice. The depiction of the Oka crisis relied on the political slant of the various journalists and media outlets that recorded, interpreted, and relayed the events. The aboriginal voice was heard shouting threats of violence because it made good "info-tainment." Eloquent calls for peace and reason went unrecorded. Justification for the anger built over generations went unrecorded.

That anger has now reached a stage of critical mass. The young are angry and tired of living in a world of internalized violence. The anger is becoming external, and the young (eighteen and under) make up 50

37

percent of the aboriginal population today. There is a time bomb in Canada—a bomb that has developed, in part, because of a lack of voice.

The lack of aboriginal voice in basic communications, in history, and in politics has created in the dominant society a series of misconceptions that mutate into indifference and racism. Nowhere in educational resource material are aboriginal people afforded their rightful place in history as builders of this country. Nor is it in the constitution; nor was it in the Meech Lake Accord. Treated by academics as a sidebar to history, aboriginal people are only referred to when their actions affect nonaboriginal people, and always from a nonaboriginal perspective. This attitude is consistent today in the media and in literature and the arts. Films, books, and accounts of aboriginal people do little more than perpetuate these misconceptions. The proud, noble "Indian" dumped on to the point of subversiveness—the pitiful victim. It's tiring, inaccurate, and makes eyes in the aboriginal community roll.

Aboriginal people have their own history, but judged by a society that doesn't share the same values and attitudes, the traditional stories are passed off as mythology. History seems to mean written history, and under that criterion the oral stories that have survived thousands of years don't hold much water. Instead, archaeologists have painted their own pictures of aboriginal history based on the existence of inanimate objects found hidden in the earth, not on the stories that are alive today.

The aboriginal voice is out there, it just isn't getting heard.

Why does a novel written by a nonaboriginal writer sell a million copies when it is riddled with stereotypes, racial attitudes, shallow, one-dimensional characters, and cultural inaccuracies? The one blatant, determining factor that will always give away the fact that an aboriginal story was not written by an aboriginal writer is that the story will be put in the context of the Judeo-Christian concern of good against evil. The aboriginal writer will create characters with more depth. Accurate portrayals involve dialogue beyond one-syllable grunting, greater insight into the issues, and consequently the presentation of viable solutions at the end. Good and evil are traded in for the aboriginal concern with balance and harmony. Avarice is a nonentity.

Critics sometimes find aboriginal literature boring and didactic. This is often in reference to stories translated into English. Stories in Inuktitut, Ojibway, MicMac, or Slave don't translate well into English, a language inadequate for the true intent of the oral story. When Cree jokes are told and those who speak English fail to find the humor, the joketeller will remark that it sounds better in Cree. Aboriginal humor by itself finds little appreciation beyond aboriginal people because it is dependent upon knowledge and appreciation of the aboriginal community. Once you understand the people, you are better capable of understanding the humor, and the philosophy.

There is a certain style to aboriginal stories that students of the Western style of drama find unpalatable. Beyond mere entertainment, the stories and the storyteller were teachers and historians. Through gestures, intonations, and elements of theater, the storyteller would captivate an audience with a tale that taught its characters lessons in the ways of the world—a world not to be treated as inanimate, but as a living, breathing being. The victory in the aboriginal story is when harmony can be achieved between the character and his or her environment. In the situation today there is a role for stories like this that is not lost on the aboriginal writer, and you cannot separate the writer from the community.

Following the summer of 1990 and the sudden awareness of aboriginal people, the fact that some wrong has been committed is accepted by most Canadians. What is not known is the true nature of that oppression and its consequences. During five hundred years of contact, the lives of aboriginal people have borne an onslaught of pain and tragedy. The result is a beleaguered, traumatized people suffering deep wounds. At present the aboriginal community is healing, and stories that reflect the struggle, and the resulting harmonious existence with a given environment, help the healing process. By their nature, aboriginal people are community oriented. Everyone in the community is part of a gigantic web that begins with the extended family, and all members of the community have the inherent responsibility to serve it. Everything must be of use, including entertainment, because to be useless is to be disgraceful. The contemporary aboriginal story puts the traditional philosophy and themes in a modern context. How we find harmony in this new, man-made environment is a common question addressed in contemporary aboriginal stories. For the survival of the community, that is the concern, and the storyteller is a member of the community.

Beyond the style of aboriginal literature and the reluctance of misconceptions to change, there is another reason that the aboriginal voice still goes unheard. The dominant society doesn't know how to listen. Grandfathers and grandmothers on First Nations across Canada always tell their grandchildren the old ways. One of those old ways is the art of listening. When someone was telling a story, when a visitor came through camp, whenever anyone had something to say, you listened. It didn't matter if they spoke for ten minutes, or if they spoke for two days, it didn't matter if they were boring or if you didn't agree with what they said, you had to listen. It was the respect afforded to anyone who wanted to speak. This attitude is lost on Western society. Attention must be grabbed and held on to. The right to speak must be fought for. The right to be heard relies on people who want to listen. If what is being said, written, or performed contradicts an already entrenched, however inaccurate, set of assumptions, it is brushed off. People are unwilling to change the misconceptions that have been driven into them by media, school textbooks, educational resource material, respected literature, films, television, and advertising. What is frustrating is that these misconceptions are based on the words and works of writers, historians, and academics who didn't come from the aboriginal perspective, but began with the same set of misconceptions that were passed on to them. So the racial stereotypes are perpetuated.

Even more damaging is that these attitudes and misconceptions reach the aboriginal population as well. Tell people that they are poor and hopeless enough times and they will begin to believe it. Today's aboriginal writers have the immense challenge of creating awareness and knowledge in not only the nonaboriginal mainstream but in the aboriginal community as well. The aboriginal voice is trying to reach two audiences—one within, and one without. It is important for aboriginal voice to reach nonaboriginal people and break down the stereotypes, but it is more important for aboriginal voice to reach aboriginal people. If the aboriginal situation is to be improved, it has to be done by aboriginal people, and that comes through having voice. Once this voice reaches the classroom, the television, the books, then comes self-awareness and self-pride, and that will be the success of the aboriginal writer/storyteller. If that voice has an impact on the mainstream, all the better, but the argument that reaching the mainstream will afford a greater financial return is of no consequence. This is why it is ludicrous for nonaboriginal writers, facing criticism for their racist portrayal of aboriginal people, to argue that aboriginal writers are merely jealous for not attaining the financial status that they have.

The racist portrayals that exist and that continue to be published work against the healing process. They are indiscriminately damaging the perception of aboriginal people. To say they must be stopped contradicts freedom of speech and the aboriginal belief that affords everyone with something to say the right to say it, but there is a responsibility that cannot be lost on the nonaboriginal writer who sets out to create a work with aboriginal characters and issues. You must be accurate.

Any writer who sets out to represent a world within the confines of a creative work must know that world if the creation is going to attain any degree of authenticity. Without it, the work will lack integrity. To write about aboriginal people requires someone who knows them, knows the culture, the history, the philosophy, and the values. One must know the cultural idiosyncrasies unique to the various aboriginal nations. To write about aboriginal people doesn't mean to write about a generic lump of people who have faced generic lumps of experience. To write about aboriginal people you must know who. Is it the Cree, the Ojibway, the Haida, the Blood, the Peigan, the Assiniboine, the Chilcotin, the Dene, the Seneca, the Onandoga, Tuscarora, Mohawk, Oneida, Cayuga, Okanagan, Squamish, Niska, Dogrib? To write about aboriginal people you must know not to use the word *Sioux,* but *Dakota, Nakota,* or *Lakota,* depending on which nation and where they live. Do not use *Eskimo;* they are Inuit. You must know that each aboriginal nation is unique and as different from another as the French from the English or the German from the Italian.

Do not write that aboriginal people started scalping, because the practice came from Europe; do not write that aboriginal people are dirty, because they bathed daily at a time when Europeans thought it unhealthy. Do not write of aboriginal people as being Indian, because that word did not come from aboriginal voice. Do not write about aboriginals within the context of Judeo-Christian ethics or the work will be riddled with contradictions.

To know and deeply understand the aboriginal experience means more than research at the library, it means living the aboriginal experience. If the nonaboriginal writer can achieve this understanding over a period of years, then the integrity of the work will speak, but the author will still be criticized for the mere fact of being nonaboriginal. In a time when the aboriginal people are more proud and angry than ever before, this criticism must be expected. As much integrity as the nonaboriginal work can achieve, it is not aboriginal voice. It is still someone speaking for aboriginal people, and this remains a serious problem. In the context of self-determination, aboriginal people must speak for aboriginal people.

Whether nonaboriginal people should write about aboriginal people is a moot question. It happens and it will continue to happen. It can only be hoped that the work will contain some degree of integrity. What is intolerable is the appropriation of the traditional stories. All too often these stories are recorded in the interest of linguistic or anthropological work, rewritten by the academic, and copyrighted in his or her name. Traditional stories are being stolen this way. There are rules and protocol regarding stories and ownership and they differ from one nation to the next. A story can be given, but only by following the existing protocol; anything less is theft. The existing copyright laws, when viewed in this light, become discriminatory because they do not consider the traditional, oral stories. These must be protected, if not by law, then by the people. Already in many parts of Canada people in the communities will no longer talk to academics. They will no longer share the stories, because like the land and its resources, everything that has been shared so far has been taken away. There is much spiritual knowledge that will not be shared for fear that it too will be stolen. As a group, the aboriginal peoples have learned not to trust.

Aboriginal people have tasted the power of voice, they have tasted pride, they have spat anger; and as the only growing population in Canada, their voice will only become stronger. As new writers emerge from the communities enriched with the traditional values and philosophies, but intrigued by the new forms of expression, a freshet of unique and dynamic literature will spread into the mainstream. This momentum is already building. Where once there was only a handful of published aboriginal writers, Canada now has an aboriginal writers association in its midst. There was a time when any dark actor could play an aboriginal role. Today, members of the aboriginal acting community boycott films and theaters that don't do justice to the integrity of aboriginal people. Aboriginal actors are calling for more scripts from aboriginal writers, and those writers are striving to answer the call. Nonaboriginal writers cannot be stopped from improperly portraying aboriginal people, but their work can be made obsolete by the shear volume of work that is rich with authenticity and integrity. The mainstream, though not knowledgeable enough yet, will soon be able to differentiate between aboriginal voice and nonaboriginal imitation. Aboriginal literature will lead the way to revolution and the emergence of aboriginal voice. Now coming in flashes, aboriginal voice will eventually be a steady stream of light that will reach everyone. If not, it will fester in frustration and the bomb of youth will detonate. Aboriginal voice will be heard one way or another. The days of the silent, proud, stoic Indian are gone, forever.

Beyond art, voice determines the survival of a people, for without voice, the people will perish. When art becomes voice, the writer/artist/ storyteller also faces the responsibility of achieving excellence within that art. New to the aboriginal community, the forms of theatre, literature, and film are being explored from the context of the aboriginal storyteller. Aboriginal art will not imitate mainstream art, but will develop into something new that will affect the mainstream. These new forms will be the successful merger of the traditional story with Western styles of art. A harmony will be achieved between the old and new and it will be something that will speak to the culture at large.

In the aboriginal way there is no good and evil, we are not sinners, and there is no fear of God. There is only the struggle to coexist peacefully. Without voice, that struggle will be lost, and so will the philosophy—a philosophy that, in examining the state of today's world, might one day save the planet.

Jordan Wheeler is a dramatist and fiction writer. He is the former editor of *Weetamah*, Manitoba's aboriginal newspaper.

Indigenous Theater

A Path toward
Cultural Empowerment

Joshua Weiser

My commitment to the development of indigenous people's theater began during my first year in Alaska, 1974. I was working as a swimming instructor in a small remote Yup'ik Eskimo village near the mouth of the Kuskoquim River. There I met a man who was 110 years old. His wife was 100. The two had been married for eighty-five years. I took a great interest in this couple, who were both in excellent health and whose minds were as sharp as a teenager's. What really caught my attention and concern were the youth of the village. I remember asking one young man if he knew much about the history of the couple. His reply, "No, I haven't taken the time, but I will someday," I found representative of young people's interest in their elders. This led me to the question of how to engage young people in taking an active interest in their cultural history; to facilitate active communication between generations that were reared to two different worlds.

Research uncovered volumes of books, video tapes, and oral recordings of elders sharing their historical knowledge and experiences. Yet little of this information was making its way into the minds of native youths. Linkage between the problem and a viable solution took place in 1978 when I attended the first Inuit Circumpolar Conference held in Point Barrow. There I witnessed the Greenlandic theater company, Tũkak' Theater, in action. Their powerful performance affected both elders and youth, briefly bridging the generations. Thus Tŭkak' inspired me to form the first Alaska native theater program in the state, Tuma Theater, through the drama department of the University of Alaska, Fairbanks.

In 1984 I was invited by my long-time friend John Pingayak to come to Chevak, a Cup'ik (Choopiik) Eskimo village located 110 miles northwest of Bethel and 10 miles inland from the Bering Sea (population 600). I was to assist him in the creation of a Cup'ik Eskimo dance/theater company, later to be named the Chevak Tanqik Theater. (Dun-gg-ik: a bright light.)

I found that the working environment was ripe for dramatic expression. For the past five years John had worked at developing both a comprehensive Cup'ik cultural heritage program and a traveling Eskimo dance troupe. Through his culture heritage program, students learn of their history, legends, language, values, subsistence and survival skills, skin sewing, tool making, traditional mask carving, and Cup'ik dance. With the cultural resources in place plus a trust relationship amongst and between me, John, and the elders of Chevak, the stage for the growth of an innovative indigenous Cup'ik theater program was set.

Let me pause here to elaborate on trust. For an outsider to enter a native village and facilitate dramatic works of any substance, a trust relationship must be built with the elders of the village. One does not just walk in and say, "OK, I'm here! Tell me a story old man. Now let's do a play about village alcohol, drug abuse, and suicide issues." It takes time to build trust; to overcome past stereotypes of non-natives. I first came to Chevak during Christmas, 1975 and spent a year immersing myself in their culture. I lived, ate, hunted, danced, took fire baths, and drank tea. Still, I had to walk through fire so to speak, in that I was accused of being a Russian spy. There were comments like, "Qussuks (white people) usually stay in the teachers' quarters. This man is not a doctor, lawyer, school teacher, postmaster, pilot, politician and he has dark brown curly hair so, he must be a spy!" I was later vindicated during a bingo game, but I tell the story to illustrate the trials one must go through sometimes in order to gain trust.

The first step in the actual work was to define the mission of the theater. What did we want to say? How and to whom? We came up with the following objectives:

1. To ensure the documentation and survival of Cup'ik history, traditional values, legends, myths, and dances.

2. To encourage the speaking and a sense of appreciation for the first language, Cup'ik.

3. To emphasize the strengths of traditional Cup'ik culture and its present-day relevance.

4. To serve as an empowerment tool; a means of elevating the self-confidence of: (a) the people of Chevak by designing performances that compliment the village as a whole; (b) the performers by providing public-speaking/theatrical communication skills and successful experiences that affirm their native identity.

5. To enlighten non-native audiences as to the issues that face indigenous peoples by promoting understanding.

6. To emphasize the need for deeper levels of communication both within our families and throughout our communities.

Next, we dealt with the question of what basic dramatic elements we wanted each piece to include. We came up with four:

1. Usage of the first language, Cup'ik.

2. Cup'ik songs and dances.

3. Audience involvement; as participants rather than observers.

4. The inclusion of a role for an elder.

Actual script development began as John and I brainstormed about various subjects. Through this process rough drafts for each script would emerge. My job was to focus the ideas from these sessions into a workable script. Constantly, through John, I would present our ideas to the elders to gain feedback, approval, and to recheck historical accuracy. For script scenes relating to social/political issues, we involved a generational cross section of the village: elders, high school and college students, single men and women, parents, and village leaders. This community involvement in the development of our scripts insured the integrity of the final product. This process also served as a reality check for me, the script writer and artistic director. Not being from Chevak, I had to be careful not to unconsciously impose my values and judgments on the people I was there to serve, else the final product would be more a non-native's interpretation of native culture than a pure indigenous people's expression.

My primary role was to listen and facilitate: to deepen levels of communication within the village and to bring to light new possibilities for dramatic expression. We wanted to show how dramatic arts can serve as a mirror in which the community can view themselves and, in the process, become aware of the unique cultural qualities that they possess. Such a mirror can reflect sensitive issues that have been taken for granted, ignored, or suppressed. We wanted to bring to light indigenous theatrical forms. These can be observed, for example, at an Eskimo dance, where movements and facial expressions convey volumes of cultural and social information, or as an elder brings a hunting experience to life with sweeping gestures, facial expressions, and an undulating voice quality, or on the banks of a river as children play with "story knives": once made of ivory, now perhaps a metal butter knife used with the spoken Cup'ik word to depict simple events in their lives with drawings in the muddy banks.

We wanted to catalyze the documentation of all aspects of Cup'ik culture. I have seen many times where a village will unconsciously take for granted the fact that their cultural history is locked within the minds of the elders. In these modern times little of this information is passed down to the younger generation. Thus with the passing of the elders, this knowledge is lost forever. In the development of scripts, questions are raised that would never have emerged before and thus the need to document becomes apparent. For these reasons we wanted to facilitate the handing down of Cup'ik cultural information to the younger generation. This is a natural process during the rehearsal phase of our scripts. The students must understand the history they are dramatizing: to claim personal ownership of this knowledge and to integrate understandings into their own lives. Chevak is ahead of most villages in that for years John Pingayak, through his cultural heritage program (which is integrated within the curriculum of Chevak's Kashunamiut School District), has been teaching this cultural knowledge to elementary and high school students.

As Tanqik Theater evolved, a natural breakdown of responsibilities emerged. John and I worked together in developing script concepts, casting parts, and in directing the final product. He took charge of Cup'ik dance choreography, the making of traditional costumes, subsistence tools, and dance masks. He also served as the prime cultural resource and elder link. My tasks, in addition to directing, included script writing, speech and drama instruction, public relations, booking, financial managment, grant writing, and travel arrangements.

In that the program was part of the school system, 90 percent of our performers (mostly high school) were drawn from the student body. Students in good academic standing could try out for various parts. Rehearsal times were usually in the evening for three-hour blocks, during which, through improvisation, the raw elements of the show jelled into something believable. During the final rehearsal stages, community members would be invited for their input.

During my five years in Chevak, John and I have produced eight major productions, toured to the Soviet Union, Australia (Expo. 88), New Zealand, Fiji, Hawaii, Washington State, Vancouver (Expo. 86), throughout Alaska, and three Alaska Fair seasons at Palmer. The following is a brief summary of our first four shows plus commentary:

New Beginnings

Deals with the dream of an elder about his people's future. Culminates in a dramatic confrontation between two masks: one of the future and one representing traditional Cup'ik culture. This, our first show, was critical to the future of the theater. We were rehearsing in the blind, not knowing what effect our show ingredients would have, especially on a non-native audience. The outcome was tremendous, especially for the cast members who, having no previous performance experience, joined with some reluctance. The success of that first performance is well represented by the words of Joe Friday, our oldest cast member (age seventy-five): "Now I know how my words can be preserved and passed on to my young people."

The Bladder Festival

An ancient ceremony of respect for the spirit within all living things, specifically the seal. It was no easy task to choreograph an ancient festival that had not taken place for some sixty years. Taking months to write, the end product is a two-and-a-half-hour experience. We trap the audience immediately. There they sit waiting to be taken into the past. The first thing they hear is heavy metal rock music to the tune of "Dirty Deeds" blasting through the sound system and a well-dressed native executive wearing headphones and bopping toward the stage. Later on stage, he admits that the pressures of the modern world and extended separation from his people has led him to alcoholism and to consider suicide. The ancient Bladder Festival is then integrated into the present as a means of spiritual healing, a means of regaining a lost identity.

Homecoming: An Alaska Native's Quest for Self-esteem

The play opens with driftwood characters bobbing in the ocean current and speculating on their futures when found by man. The scene is interrupted by an audience plant, a member of the theater, who declares the actions on stage to be irrelevant to present-day Alaska native issues. We've had police, security, and even audience members try to restrain our plant and throw him out, thus adding to the audience participation dynamics of our plays. The scene works so well that at the plays conclusion many audience members are still unsure about the identity of the "disturbed young man." Again, as with the Bladder Festival, the play seeks to heal the spirit of this torn character and return him to a place of balance and self-respect.

Homesick for My Dream

This piece is based upon the experience of a Chevak student (Pingayak's daughter) who spent seven days living in a pre-contact environment. The program is called the Kashunamiut Project, where students gain an appreciation for the life-style of their parents and elders by actually living as they did a hundred years in the past. The dream she had in an actual sod house at the site speaks of her people losing their language, their culture, their self-respect by depending on welfare checks, getting brainwashed by cable television, and forgetting how to communicate with their families. The play graphically contrasts a historically close relationship to the land with the pressures brought on by a cash economy. Audience participation is engaged at the onset when the cast goes seal hunting in the audience. One (preselected) audience member is harpooned, brought on stage, and skinned alive (so to speak).

The Kashunamiut Project

The Kashunamiut Project was actually an outgrowth of Tanqik Theater. John became aware that teaching Cup'ik culture for forty-five minutes, five days a week, in a modern classroom was not sufficient time for his students to truly understand what life was like for their parents and ancestors. He concluded that the teaching environment and time period had to be changed. To correct the situation, a total cultural immersion concept was implemented. Located at a traditional hunting site twenty miles from Chevak, a pre-contact village (named Kashunamiut) was built during the summer of 1988.

This "new" village came to life by choreographing the memories of our village elders. These memories were "taught" to village members who were hired to play the role of an ancient family. For the older members, memory rekindling is a better term. During the winter months, this pre-contact family adopts high school students from Chevak and area villages for a seven-day period. The break in time is complete in that there is no contemporary reference, either oral or visual. Only the first language, Cup'ik Eskimo is spoken. The week's activities are those that would have constituted life during that month fifty to a hundred years ago.

By living the life-style of their parents and ancestors, the members of Kashunamiut leave with a greater appreciation for their culture, a perspective on the effects of modern influences, and a renewed sense of spirituality and personal worth. Thus, Chevak Tanqik Theater has directly (or indirectly) inspired a cultural renaissance for the people it was meant to represent; a means to reestablish a connection to the land, and to preserve and pass on traditional Cup'ik culture to the younger generation. In this connection Kashunamiut has become the perfect "script generator," an ideal environment for the formation of new performance directions and concepts.

Joshua Weiser is founder of the Tuma Native Theater, University of Alaska, Fairbanks, and of the Chevak Tanqiq Theater. He teaches theater arts throughout the Fairbanks North Star Borough School District.

II
Scripts

Images from "Inuit," performed by the Tũkak' Theater: Rasmus Lybert, Naja Qeqe, and Anda Kristiansen. Photograph by Ole Jørgensen.

Images from "Inuit": Makka Kleist. Photograph by Ole Jørgensen.

Inuit–The People

A performance text created by Reidar Nilsson and the Tūkak' Theater Ensemble

Translated from the Danish by Per K. Brask

Characters

The names Bent, Laila, Else, and Kent are the names of actual cast members.

TORNAQ QAQORTOQ: The white spirit.

AMO: A familiar spirit of assistance to a sorcerer; has a large head, almost no body, and very long arms.

AMAGAIAT: A horrible old troll living in the mountains, where she takes travelers by surprise and devours them.

AJUMAQ: A very unpleasant spirit; has a dog's head and a human body and everything it touches rots and perishes.

TORNARSUUK: The chief among familiar spirits. Whatever the other familiar spirits can't do Tornarsuuk can. He lives a solitary and fearless life.

INUNERUP ARNA: The mother of the sea, who lives on the ocean floor. The evil deeds of mankind appear as dirt in her hair.

Images from "Inuit": Makka Kleist, Maariu Olsen, and Aqqa Brummersted Olsen. Photograph by Ole Jørgensen.

Images from "Inuit": Anda Kristiansen, Makka Kleist, Maariu Olsen, Qisu Alaufsen, Aqqa Brummersted Olsen, Rassi Thygesen. Photograph by Ole Jørgensen.

Images of "Inuit," from a performance in Greenland: Bendo Schmidt, Naja Qeqe, Soré Møller, Qisu Alaufsen. Photograph by Ole Jørgensen.

Prologue

BENT: A long, long time ago
before my father's grandfather was born
—people used to be together
—they lived together
—they played together and they laughed
—they loved one another
One person told the next
about those days
and about the times that followed

THAT'S HOW STORIES ARE BORN
Embedded in our stories
are the experiences of people
so they don't always tell
of beautiful things

But it isn't possible
to adorn a story
just to make it
comfortable for the listener
if it is to remain true

Your tongue must echo
what
is to be described
You must not adjust your story
to the taste and temperament of
your listener

No one should lend credence
to the words of a new-born
but there is truth in
the experiences of older generations

When we tell our legends
we don't speak about ourselves

It is the wisdom of those who came before us
which speaks through us

ALL: tivanijorpunga iliunula
      issiqiunula
      issitaja-papataja
      nungup avatane
      issiqissa upapaqissa
      pinerninguaq tingujamarpat
      pinarisanguarput

In Greenland
an old children's game
has been passed down through the years
from child to child

nanumi-i qitornaqarni-i
qinernertarparmio-o
nano-nano
nano-ija

When your child is a bear
you have to care for it
and watch out
nano-nano
nano-ija

Then it happened . . .

(The suppression of the individual begins.)

BENT: Enough is enough!
      (The lament of the women begins and it lasts until Laila gets caught. Kent is caught and a mask and clothes are put on him. Laila is caught and has a mask put on her. She is tempted by Tornaq Qaqortoq. She falls to her knees and crawls up to him.)

LAILA: Uhm, I smell the smell of a real man!
       Master, I am your slave!

Use me!
Make use of me!

The ceremony:

(*There is humming during the ceremony. When Else is dressed and ready the humming stops.*)

BENT: Listen to my proclamation
There is only one God:
PROGRESS

In the holy name of PROGRESS
I proclaim:

That the people are no longer *a* people
but a population

that individuals are
no longer free
they are slaves

In the holy name of PROGRESS
You are MY SLAVES
(*The people are forced into a frenzied dance of madness. They dance their way into the realm of fear—where one's soul is easily lost.*)

Nauk ukua inuit? (Where are the people?)

(*After the dance people collapse on the verge of total exhaustion. A question is heard repeated over and over:*)
WHERE IS THE INDIVIDUAL?
(*And the same two answers are repeated over and over:*)
THE INDIVIDUAL IS DEAD!
YOU ARE MY SLAVES!

ELSE: (*alone on the floor*)
My soul, where are you hidden?

Let me come and get you.
Have you fled south of those
who live to the south of us?
Let me come and get you.

My soul, where are you hidden?
Let me come and get you.
Have you fled east of those
who live to the east of us?
Let me come and get you.

My soul, where are you hidden?
Let me come and get you.
Have you fled north of those
who live to the north of us?
Let me come and get you.

My soul, where are you hidden?
Let me come and get you.
Have you fled west of those
who live to the west of us?
Let me come and get you.

My soul, where are you hidden?
Have you fled far away from us?
Have you gone away past those
who live way past us?
Let me come and get you.

My soul, where are you?
All spirits listen to me!
My soul is lost!
Help me!
Help me!
(*In answer the helpful spirit Amo appears. He bends down to help
Else exit.*)

AMO: I will help you
    I shall help you

The spirit came . . .

(. . . *from the realm of the ancient ones. Amo promises to make
the dangerous journey down to the world of the spirits.*)

AMO: Here I stand
humbly
my arms stretched out

Spirit of the air
come
come quickly!
Amo calls you!

Spirit of the mountain
come
come quickly!
Amo calls you!

Spirit of the sea
come
come quickly!
Amo calls you!

Here I stand
humbly
my arms stretched out
asking for help
on behalf of
the human soul
(*Amo is attacked by Amagaiat.*)

AMAGAIAT: Who are you who dares to make
the lonely journey to the kingdom of the spirits?

AMO: I am the spirit Amo.

AMAGAIAT: I don't know you
and I don't like
your huge head.

AMO: Don't chase me away!
Don't kill me!
I'm looking for INUNERUP ARNA
to help find the human soul.

AMAGAIAT: Your head is so fleshy—
your bottom too!
I think I'll make soup
for dinner.

AMO: No, please don't!
Show me the way to your mother.
Help me to help
the human soul. (*Amo manages to get free, but not for long.
Ajumaq attacks.*)

AJUMAQ: Hey,
Fat head!
And who are you?

AMO: I'm looking for INUNERUP ARNA
to help find the human soul.

AJUMAQ: I don't trust
people with arms as long as yours.
I wonder what you're up to.

AMO: Believe me, please! I'm looking for help
to find the human soul.

AJUMAQ: I'll cut your
long arms and your fat head
into tiny, tiny pieces—
and then I'll take them along to the sea
as a present to her.

AMO: No, please don't touch me
  show me the way to your mother.
  (*Ajumaq remains unpleasant. Amo finally manages to chase him
  away. Amo then collapses, exhausted. Tornarsuuk comes to his
  rescue.*)

TORNARSUUK: He can still make it.
  ENOUGH'S ENOUGH
  Amagaiat—come here!
  You and your brother
  will take Amo to your mother.

AMAGAIAT: Brother—brother!
  Do you think we should help the spirit Amo?

AJUMAQ: I wonder if a human being is the
  right place for a soul to reside?

AMAGAIAT: Many of them are quite good.

AJUMAQ: They probably just lost their way
  on the journey.
  The people can't know themselves any longer
  because their souls have lost their way.

AMAGAIAT: Let's ask mother.
  (*Amagaiat and Ajumaq run to Inunerup Arna.*)

AMAGAIAT/AJUMAQ: Mother—mother
  INUNERUP ARNA.

AJUMAQ: A spirit called Amo has
  arrived—he says he's a messenger from the people.

AMAGAIAT: He's got a head the size of the moon
  and as black as the night . . .

AJUMAQ: And arms long like this . . .

INUNERUP ARNA: What does he want?

AJUMAQ: To ask for help to find their souls.

AJUMAQ: He wants to talk to you . . .

AMAGAIAT: To ask for your help.
(*After more teasing by Amagaiat and Ajumaq, Inunerup Arna goes to meet Tornarsuuk.*)

INUNERUP ARNA: Who are you?
How dare you come here?
What do you want?

TORNARSUUK: Oh, great mother,
I am Tornarsuuk.
The people have lost their way.
The people have lost their way.
They have lost their way
they have lost their souls.
They are in pain and agony
—they find no rest
—they find no happiness in life.

INUNERUP ARNA: Who sent you down here?

TORNARSUUK: Someone who hasn't quite
lost his soul.
Oh, great mother
Inunerup Arna
come with me to the world
of the people
and show them where
they can recover
their souls.

INUNERUP ARNA: Very well!
Lead me to them!

TORNARSUUK: This way!
    Come!
    Follow me!
    This way!
    Come!
    Come!

The Dance of Life.

(*Inunerup Arna is led to the world of the people where she shows in a fiery dance how the people can get rid of their masks.*)

INUNERUP ARNA: The great ocean
    sets me in motion
    The great ocean
    starts me moving!

    It moves me
    like algae on a stone
    in a stream.

    The arc of the heavens
    sets me in motion.
    The forceful winds
    blow through my wind.

    They pull me along
    till I tremble from joy.

    Let joy chase away sorrow!
    Let joy chase away the mask!

    Human—Give life its life!
    Human—Give life its life!

    Let darkness fall away!

    The darkness is gone!

(After the cast has removed their masks joy prevails. Suddenly Tornaq Qaqortoq shows up. Laila yells:)

LAILA: TORNAQ QAQORTOQ!

THE WOMEN: *(to Kent)* Move behind him.
Surprise him from the back!
(They run up to the white spirit:)
White spirit—follow us!

(Kent sneaks up on him from the back and attacks. There is a fight.)

In life struggle is necessary . . .

The End

Gesat

A play by Nils Gaup
and Knut Walle

Translated from the Norwegian
by Per K. Brask

THE STUDENT: Good evening and welcome to our show. My name is Pedersen and I'm a student. Let's get right to the point. In the beginning of the century we're currently on our way out of, two noteworthy Sami artists lived in Kristiania, the capital of Norway. One of them was Matti Aikio. He was from Karasjok and he was the first Sami writer to write in Norwegian. He wrote seven books, two of which are still quite well known. They are *Dressed in Animal Hide* and *The Settlement at the Riverbank*. They are both set in Karasjok. So, perhaps one could say that the tracks left by Aikio have mainly been swept away. Still, we have to acknowledge that when he was alive he was clearly part of the scenery. He didn't only write novels; he was also very prolific in newspapers and magazines, writing about all sorts of things: defense, religious matters, the Sami. He produced quite an extensive commentary to Einstein's theory of relativity, and he solved the problem of trisecting the square—which is mathematically impossible but Aikio did it. Well, as a student it is my job to leaf through the old books and documents and try to develop a clear picture of their author. Who was Aikio, the phenomenon Matti Aikio? To find the answer I thought we might turn the clock back to 1910 and invite Aikio to come and answer a few simple questions. Matti Aikio!

MATTI: Yes, I am, indeed, the first Norwegian author of . . . Lapp heritage. There were authors before me but they only wrote in Lapp. In Kristiania where I live they call me Boccaccio Borealis, which means Boccaccio from the far north. If any of you thinks that is some sort of pub or dance hall, say in Tromsø, you are quite mistaken. Boccaccio was the first European author and depictor of the life of the people. And I am Boccaccio Borealis! No applause? (*There's applause.*) Thank you! Thank you very much! I was born in Karasjok in 1872 and I lived there till I was sixteen, when I moved to Vadsø to attend the county school there . . . isn't that correct Mr. Student?

THE STUDENT: Yes, it is. (*He checks his papers just in case.*)

MATTI: At that time my knowledge of the Norwegian language was very limited. When I heard the word *house* or something like that I would know that it referred to a house . . . or something like that. Even when as a grown man I took my secondary exams I would confuse the words in Norwegian for "message" and "master." The essay topic we were given was "Write about the harvest." And I wrote with great unction about "the servant girls leading the bellowing gentry down from the mountain to the settlement."

THE STUDENT: So, you arrived in Kristiania in 1896—twenty-four years old. How did you adapt to this new life?

MATTI: How did I adapt . . . ha, ha . . . uhm . . . ahhh youth. I think I studied law for a while and I taught here and there. I was also working on a play which stayed so long in my suitcase that it shriveled like moldy bread. But later I turned it into a novel the title of which I won't reveal in order to protect my good name.

THE STUDENT: *King Akab.*

MATTI: I beg your pardon?

THE STUDENT: *King Akab and Nabot's Vineyard.* Copenhagen 1904. Alexander Brandt Publishers, Denmark. Correct?

MATTI: Uhmm . . . Yes . . . Yes I think so. In Denmark was it? A first attempt I'd call it. (*Quickly.*) My real debut was *Dressed in Animal Hide,* which was published in 1906 by the largest publishing house in Norway—Aschehoug. In all due humility I brought a few of the reviews. (*They bulge out of his pockets.*) I would like to start reading from the one which appeared in *Dagbladet.* (*He begins to read.*)

THE STUDENT: Thank you, thank you very much, Aikio. I have all the reviews right here. I have . . .

MATTI: (*Jumps down from the stage and gives the review to someone in the audience.*) Please! Read it to your friends and acquaintances and then pass it on . . . Thank you! (*He gets back on stage.*) I'm sorry. Where were we?

THE STUDENT: I'd like to ask a couple of questions about King Akab, or rather, about Napoleon.

MATTI: Napoleon?!

THE STUDENT: You had some difficulties getting that book published. I have here the letter you wrote to the Danish publisher about it. (*He reads.*) "I am well known in Kristiania. My name is recognized from the newspapers as I have written several articles for *Aftenposten* and *Verdens Gang.* I am the first and only university student of Finnish-Lapp heritage in Norway, although I am perhaps better known for my striking resemblance to Napoleon." And so on. My attention was also caught by a small passage in the book itself. There is a scene in which the protagonist, the student Fløiberg, stands in front of the mirror examining his face. It says: (*He reads.*) "If only you could cut away those disfiguring mongolian features which stand out like weeds at the expense of my noble roman lines. I wonder if it would hurt. This part would have to go, and this too—then add a little there. Then it would be like looking at, Goddammed, it would be like looking at Napoleon!" Both the protagonist in this story and you yourself seem strangely preoccupied with Napoleon. So, the obvious question is whether there are other similarities?

MATTI: And the answer is simple. Fløiberg is Fløiberg and Aikio is Aikio. Besides, I can assure you that that novel is of little interest. *Dressed in Animal Hide,* my debut, on the other hand . . .

THE STUDENT: Hold on Aikio. I want to zero in on this question about your Lapp Heritage. It confuses me, you see.

MATTI: Why?

THE STUDENT: To begin with you stated earlier that your background is Sami. In the letter I just read from, you wrote that you were of Finnish-Lapp heritage. Somewhere else you've written that your mother's Germanic appearance is due to her Swedish blood. In addition you want to look like Napoleon?! I find that very confusing!

MATTI: How could anyone blame me for looking like Napoleon. (*He produces a portrait which is simultaneously projected onto a screen.*) Look. Is that Napoleon or not?!

THE STUDENT: Granted. But who are you really? Are you Sami, Finnish, Swedish, or Germanic or . . . to put it in a different way: Who do you identify yourself with?

MATTI: Aha, identity! I identify mainly with . . . with . . . with . . . with him! (He points to his portrait.)

THE STUDENT: That is with Napoleon.

MATTI: Napoleon?! Ha, ha, ha. No, no, my dear friend. Don't be such a pushover. That's not Napoleon, it just looks like him. That's Matti Aikio. Napoleon is Napoleon, Fløiberg is Fløiberg, and Aikio is Aikio. Understand?

THE STUDENT: I have a few other pictures of you here. (*He shows a flattering caricature from* Dagbladet.)

MATTI: That couldn't possible be . . . Is that me?

THE STUDENT: It is. What about this one? Do you feel better portrayed in this one? (*He shows a caricature where Aikio is caricatured very unflatteringly.*)

MATTI: Damned . . . That was a rather embarrassing story that!

THE STUDENT: I have that embarrassing story right here. (*He begins to read.*)

MATTI: (*He discreetly tries to stop the student.*)

THE STUDENT: (*Reads.*) "Once Matti Aikio stayed in Copenhagen for a few weeks. When he returned he bragged about his fortune with the women there which he achieved by confiding in them—one after the other—that Nature had endowed the Sami with particularly impressive sexual equipment." Shall I go on?

MATTI: There is no need to go into the details of that particular episode.

THE STUDENT: Very well, let's return to the drawing, then. It's a pity we don't have it in color.

MATTI: What's your point?

THE STUDENT: Your nose . . . (*The nose on the drawing is darkened to indicate a different color.*)

MATTI: Oh, you're insinuating that if the drawing had been in color the nose would have been red. No, the whole thing was a big misunderstanding. I was on my way home from the Theatre Cafe one night—that's the cafe in Kristiania most frequented by artists. There was a blizzard, the wind was howling through the street. So, I decided to stay overnight inside a snowdrift. I'd done that often as a boy in Karasjok. I dug my way into the first and best snowdrift I found by the curb of the road and fell asleep very quickly. After I'd slept for a while, I noticed someone pinching my nose. I woke up and saw a gentleman standing there poking at my nose with his cane. I got angry and screamed: Leave my nose alone! I've camped for the night! The guy apologized saying that he'd mistaken my nose for a cigar butt burning in the snow, and that he'd tried to extinguish it! But my nose is surely not so red that you'd mistake it for a burning cigar butt. (*To the audience*) Or, is it? (*He nods pleasantly to a beautiful woman in the audience.*) Thank you very much. No, I have always waged a serious fight against fire water . . .

THE STUDENT: (*He takes out a few photocopies and quotes.*) " . . . and I have suffered several great . . ."

MATTI: (*Peeks at the papers.*) . . . defeats. I see. So, that's how I put it? Yes, there may have been a few defeats, but by God, it was fun, boy.

THE STUDENT: Maybe we should talk about *Dressed in Animal Hide,* after all. The title—*Dressed in Animal Hide*—isn't intended to be slightly suggestive, titillating, is it? I could well imagine that the decent folk of the capital might envision scenes of the most marvelous primitive forms of sensual goings on when they saw that title. After which they'd run to the nearest book shop in a state of forbidden joy.

MATTI: *Dressed in Animal Hide* simply refers to being dressed in reindeer skins. You should try it sometime in minus forty or fifty degrees and no bear in the woods would be better off than you!

THE STUDENT: I have no doubt. But you also changed your name when this novel was published. From Mathias Isacksen as you were known previously to Matti Aikio—a more Sami sounding name. Isn't that a little conspicuous?

MATTI: Aikio is my father's name. I have every right to that name. I am a Lapp, Goddamnit! Young man, it appears to me that you are trying to suggest that I exploit the fact that I am a Lapp at cocktail parties, while at the same time denying it in some other context. Well, this too, is of little importance. No, my sense of reality is too great for me to feel any happiness or any sense of pride because I am a Lapp. My sense of belonging in Norway is not something I've built up slowly and superficially over the years. No, I've felt

that since I was a child. I remember that we kids in Karasjok—
and we were brave like nobody else—we looked down on the
Finnish Lapps on the other side of the river Tana. And we didn't
hesitate giving expression to our contempt. We were Norwegians,
part of the free Norway.

THE STUDENT: In that case what about the main character in *Dressed in
Animal Hide?* Jussa. He is Sami and he is deeply in love with
Norwegian Elna. Here is a section from the book in which he
stands atop a grove and peers down over the church hill. It says:
(*He reads.*) "Once more she appeared. Her hair was golden and it
shone in the sunlight. She was so tall, so light and so erect. And
he thought: The people down there reach for the light and subjugate
the earth. The people here flee towards darkness and destruction."
End of quote. One could probably say about Jussa that he not only
doesn't feel particularly proud to be Sami. He even feels inferior.

MATTI: That's not uncommon.

THE STUDENT: But you don't share this problem?

MATTI: *Mein Gott!* The Germanic peoples surrounded the Finnmark a
long time ago and they are intent on planting the seeds of modern
culture over the whole area. What use is it to stand moping in the
bushes? In fact, I don't think that's what the Lapps of the interior
Finnmark are going to do.

THE STUDENT: The Lapps of the interior Finnmark, you say. In your third
book *Ginungagap* we meet the coastal Sami. I would like you to
read a little to us from that book. Especially, the section about
Pollacked-Erke.

MATTI: (*Reads.*) One summer Pollacked-Erke settled by the sea and began
fishing for pollack. He ate pollack day in and day out until he
turned yellow, brown, and greasy from his toes to the tuft of hair
between his shoulders, which is why he was called Pollacked-
Erke. Pollacked-Erke got up and headed for Elias's place. He took
short, quiet, and quick steps, as if he were on important business.
That was his manner of walking. Elias could see his smile from

Matti reads to the student: Nils Gaup and Knut Walle. Photograph by
Ola Røe.

far away. "Hello Pollacked-Erke," said Elias. As usual, Pollacked-
Erke let out a melancholy, growling whine. Then his words followed, slowly and methodically. He spoke almost confessionally.
"Elias, might I try on your boots." Elias invited him in to try on
the boots. When he got them on and had taken a few steps across
the floor he felt literally moved by the spirit. The filthy tuft of hair
protruded from its usual hiding place between his shoulders: "This
is wonderful! I can feel the joints in my feet, in the bottom of my

feet! Please, Elias, may I try on your sweater?" He put on the sweater, a vest and pair of trousers, but the trousers were so long that they folded in a zigzag down over his crooked legs. "When I go out now, everyone will think I'm the minister!" And then he strolled out and down toward the huts. "Look, look dáža" a group of Lapp kids yelled out and surrounded him in great joy. "Look dáža! Are you a minister dáža? Soon the entire village had gathered around Pollacked-Erke in great jubilation. "Where does Pollacked-Erke live?" asked the minister. "He lives here in that hut," the kids yelled. And the kids and everyone else squealed with pleasure. "I will go and see him and thank him for his hospitality. Who will be my interpreter? How will I get into this cave? I can't find the door. Boy, find the door! I see some light now. What a stench! Can a person really live here? There's a fire on the floor! Kelp and fish heads in a pot over the fire! A small hole in the roof!! And not a single window?! I can't even stand up, the hut is so low. Dry the provisions box with a cloth so I can sit down! Oh, phew, the kid's filthy, they are all filthy. Smoke and sour air!!" But, later when they were all gathered in the yard Pollacked-Erke was preoccupied by his son, who was almost ten years old. He was a wonderful miracle of a kid. He was light, handsome, and huge. Pollacked-Erke was measuring him for the fourth or fifth time. "He's growing," he said, "one fine day his head'll grow straight through the smoke vent and he'll walk away with the hut around his neck like a bear's collar!"

THE STUDENT: Isn't it slightly prejudicial to write about people that way?

MATTI: Please, it's certainly not my intention to say anything pejorative about the coastal Lapps. They are merely the victims of a fate which relocated them to a strange environment. I think it's sad that these yellowish brown beings are the first and often the only impression tourists have of the Lapps.

THE STUDENT: You have some knowledge of the coastal Sami, then?

MATTI: I will never forget the first time I was in a Lapp hut, which I found in an out-of-the-way inlet. I wasn't from Hønefoss or from

Lillestrøm, I was from Karasjok, but it made me shudder nonetheless.

THE STUDENT: I have the *Aftenposten's* review of the book right here.
(*He reads.*) "Aikio's previous novel, *Dressed in Animal Hide,*
received well-deserved attention. But there is a limit to originality.
In *Ginungagap* the young author really reveals the barbarian. . . .
He writes passionately about conditions in the North and about its
people who seem in greater need of missionary work than either
the Basques or the Zulus. What Aikio lacks most is self-control.
He lets his passions carry him away to the extent that he seems to
disappear far underneath that animal hide he should by now have
rid himself of."

MATTI: I do realize that I suffered a defeat with that book. But how would
Norwegian critics be able to assess the conditions I described?
And when you attempt to depict reality you cannot help but show
some of its more unflattering aspects.

THE STUDENT: But there are also . . .

MATTI: I should have written it in Lapp! It's so difficult to write in a
language other than your own. But it's not just a question of the
language. It's about what's in your blood. Your race sets certain
limits for you. You'll never be able to cross them. Not really.
Look at the Jews. They have nothing to keep them together,
nothing which their entire race would fight for, they stagnate.
They stagnate materialistically. It is this stagnation rather than
their qualities as a race which makes them despised by other
peoples. I arrived in Hamburg just as there was a congress of Jews
gathering to formulate the goal of returning to Palestine to take
back the land of their fathers. These Jews were treated with quite
a different respect than other Jews. Just walking into a cafe you'd
notice the difference. And I thought to myself: It's because they
have an idea to fight for, a development to strive for. When the
process of stagnation ends so does the contempt.

THE STUDENT: Why don't you write a book about issues like that?

MATTI: I am. But it's very difficult.

THE STUDENT: Is it about the Sami?

MATTI: The Sami? I call it *The Son of a Hebrew*, it's about the Jews! Thank you very much! (*To the audience.*) Thank you for your attention! (*He exits.*)

THE STUDENT: That was the Sami author, Matti Aikio. Ten years later, in 1920, another Sami arrived in Kristiania. He came down to become an artist. His name was John Andreas Savio.

Music. The following text appears on the screen:
John Andreas Savio   born 1902
change to:

Sara (sister)	born 1903	died 1903
Sara Elise (sister)	born 1905	died 1905
Else (mother)		died 1905
Per (father)		died 1905

change to:
His father drowned in the Varanger Fjord on his way to pick up a coffin for his wife. John was three years old.

(During the following monologue slides of some of John Savio's paintings are shown. The text is written in response to his paintings.)

JOHN: (*Enters.*) There's one episode I remember particularly well from my childhood at Bugøyfjord! It was Fall. A friend and I were on our way to a pond to pick up some peat. A sheet of shining ice covered the pond—it glittered in the sun like a diamond. I was so taken by this sight that I immediately began to scratch figures into the surface of the ice. I created the most fantastical figures. Suddenly my friend came skating right across my drawings. I got so angry that I was about to attack him. Then it dawned on me that perhaps he hadn't seen my drawings. I still wonder about that. If you want to create something you'll have to learn to bear that those who can't see your work may step on it out of ignorance.

I grew up in my grandparents' house in Bugøyfjord and I went to school at Vardø. Isak Saba was my teacher. He became the first Sami in parliament. He was an erudite and wise man with an undying love for our people. He introduced me to hard political realities and our position in them. He also introduced me to that for which there are no words—the special note which is the sound of the harmony which has existed for thousands of years between people and Nature in Sami country.

After two years in Vardø I had to move to Borkenes to finish secondary school. It was the creeping disease of consumption which forced me down into milder climes. After that I went to Bodø, and then on to Kristiania to take my diploma. That was in 1920 and I began studying at the School of Fine Arts at the same time. But my illness prevented me from finishing my studies. I was admitted to the hospital in 1921 with consumption and pneumonia. The room was white and I was drenched in sweat. Fear of death had begun to invade me. I felt more helpless than ever. But in spite of all that, I tried to read books about the great masters: Munch, Domier, Dürer and about Japanese wood carvings. Suddenly a nurse entered. She looked serious, but said nothing. She sat down by my bed and she began to pray for me. I thought the doctors had given up on me and that I was really about to die. In this confrontation with death one thing was clear in my mind: I cannot and I will not die now. A difficult time followed but I knew that I had something important to do in life.

Soon things turned around for the better. They removed one of my lungs and I could be released. My body was weak, however, and I was not really able to work. But inside I was burning more than ever. And from then on I devoted myself completely to my art. I practiced drawing every day—I strove for perfection. Possessed, I looked for the message of my art.

In the tension between the ocean of light in the summertime and the eternal darkness of winter lies the hum of that special note—the note which provides the unique qualities of our minds— humankind in struggle and in harmony with Nature—from expressions of the most ecstatically wild to the gentlest of caresses. The lazy attitude of a Sunday morning does not belong here. But people look for the easy way out—that's why danger lurks ahead for our people. The expectation of ruin—the fear that we will lose our identity haunts us. At times everything seems lost.

THOUGHT—which the one who created us implanted in our minds—and TRUST in other thinking beings have taken away our aggression. This makes us vulnerable, easy prey, much too vulnerable and fearful of anything which seems inhuman and aggressive.

But we will always live in HOPE. And we will always DREAM of finding the calm harmony of life. A summer evening when everything is at peace, everything is unreal—a dream world—all quiet. A dawn where everything is waking up.

HOPE also lies hidden in the dreamy eyes of a Sami girl. Among our people women have always been held in high regard. She represents life and warmth. Abruptly we were torn from the dream and we stand at the border. The border between the effective new culture on one side and our Sami identity on the other. Those who cut the roots to their own culture and run away from themselves into the other culture abuse the very core of their beings and they become like a birch tree which has grown even taller without nourishment. Its sickly trunk is thin and without sap. Its leaves are pale green and hang. This can also happen to the Sami who turns his back on his heritage. Especially to the Sami who has moved ahead and been successful—he who feels raised above the rest of his tribe and looks down on them. At the same time, however, he has become hopeless in a strange culture—he has become uncertain and weak.

But in the past when the threat of extinction reared its head our forefathers looked it straight in the face—calmly and confidently—without fear of the new times. And they survived because of their uniqueness.

The land of the Sami is like Norway while she was ruled by Denmark—we are sleeping a cultural sleep. By seeking our inner strength, finding the identity of our heritage, we can assert our right to exist and wake up from our sleep.

THE STUDENT: I don't know whether those two ever met, even though they lived in Norway's capital at the same time. One could speculate on what would have happened if they had. Together with some Sami friends we in fact did speculate on this. We will now move almost ten years closer to our own time as we move to the year 1929. John Savio was twenty-seven years old then and suffered badly from consumption. Matti Aikio was fifty-seven years old, that is thirty years older than Savio. He had his own problems. We now move to Oslo in 1929; the capital had changed its name in 1924. The setting is at St. Olav's Hotel, St. Olav's Street, Oslo. 1929.

MATTI: (*Reading a letter*) "We are therefore unable to advance you the amount requested . . ." (*He crumbles the paper and throws it in the wastepaper basket.*) Amazing that a serious publisher is unable to understand . . . that you can't write a novel without a roof over your head. Not to mention that the greatest disadvantage of writing outdoors in the winter is that the ink freezes and your fingers grow numb . . . (*picks up a card and writes*) I am under the impression that you are harassing me over a few thousand, a sum which to me is like mere pennies. Don't you realize that I am Napoleon's grandson? (*He is about to go and mail it but he changes his mind.*) The hotel manager may well show up with the bill any moment now . . . Unless a miracle happens it looks like old Matti must once again dig himself into a snowdrift. (*There's a knock on the door. Matti freezes.*) Come in.

JOHN: Buore beaivvi! [Hello!]

MATTI: John Savio!

JOHN: Heive go boahtit sisa? [May I come in?]

MATTI: Of course. Come in, come in! I never thought we'd meet again. It's been a long time. (*He slaps John on the back.*)

JOHN: (*Coughs.*)

MATTI: I see you've still got the illness . . .

JOHN: Mun lean mannáme davás ihttin, ja mun ipmirdin . . . ahte lei odne . . . don sáhtet máksit munnje dien vealggi . . . [I'm going up north tomorrow. It was my understanding . . . that . . . you'd be able to pay me back . . . today . . .]

MATTI: Oh yes, the money I owe you . . . Yes, of course . . . yes.

JOHN: Mon livčcen galgan leat davvin juo áiga . . . juo . . . dat lei dušše dat . . . [I should have gone north a long time ago . . . yes . . . that's all.]

MATTI: I see, you're leaving this glorious Parnassus tomorrow already?! Why such a hurry?

JOHN: Mon lean [I have] . . . Some friends have agreed to meet me, so I'll have to be off.

MATTI: (*Makes John sit down.*) No, no, calm down. Don't be in such a rush. You have to remember that you're here in the capital in order to refine yourself. You'll meet other artists here. You'll study the masters and find the key to art's . . . (*He stops abruptly. Listens. Did he hear footsteps?*)

JOHN: To give life to my paintings, as you say, I have to go to where there are appropriate subjects for them. My paintings . . .

MATTI: (*Interrupting*) John, listen. I'm expecting my publisher at any minute. I have to make a fair copy of a section for him to read. Could I see you a little later?

JOHN: Mon fereten rahkanit . . . jus mei sahtaseime dal . . .

MATTI: (*Interrupting.*) That's a little difficult right now. I have to go to the bank and . . . But let's meet at the Theatre Cafe at (*He takes out a pocket watch from his vest; only the chain, however, is left.*) six o'clock?

JOHN: Well, if that's the only way, then . . .

MATTI: It's a date! I'll see to it that you get your money. I promise.

JOHN: I'll see you at six, then.

MATTI: At six o'clock. (*There's a knock on the door. Matti freezes.*)

JOHN: Perhaps that's your publisher?

MATTI: Sshhh . . . (*loudly*) Just a minute! (*He takes John's bag and his hat and makes him sit down.*) Come in!

THE HOTEL MGR: Well, Matti, here's your bill . . . Rather hefty . . . It's for three months . . . It isn't . . .

MATTI: (*Interrupts discretely. Quietly.*) I'm just in the middle of a conversation with my publisher . . . we're very near a conclusion. Could we take care of this a little later? I will call on you as soon as we've dotted the i's and crossed the t's. We're almost done.

THE HOTEL MGR: I'm so sorry, I wasn't aware . . . You'll call on me no later than five o'clock then, so we can finish this matter *today*. (*to John*) Excuse me, sir . . . (*He exits.*)

JOHN: (*Looks at Matti. Matti keeps standing for a while. A long embarrassing pause. Matti lies down on his bed.*)

MATTI: So, there you had a little peek behind the scenes in the life of the great Matti Aikio. An author whose manuscripts an entire world is awaiting with bated breath while the publishers bid furiously against each other to get the rights to publish them. (*He laughs.*) We could drink to that if only I had something to offer. (*Pause.*) I'm in debt to the entire world. Ten kroner here, fifteen kroner there, a hundred, five hundred, a thousand . . . John, please don't be angry with me. (*John doesn't answer.*) Things are going from bad to worse, John. I have no money to give you. I'm not worthy of your friendship.

JOHN: Dus i leat ruhta . . . de daja dan dalán. [If you haven't any money . . . then say so.]

MATTI: I don't get anything done . . . How am I supposed to write when I have to engage in this enervating life of a beggar all the time. Why am I not awarded any grants? My situation is completely desperate.

JOHN: Mon in jáhke leat du ruhtaváttisvuoðat, dahje viina, dahje eara mohkohallamat mi ráfehuhta du barggu—muhtu dus i gávdno iešdovdu. [I don't think that it's financial problems or alcohol or any other excuse that's blocking your work—your problem is that you don't have any self-respect.]

MATTI: I beg your pardon?

JOHN: Dus i gávdno iešdovdu. [You have no self-respect.]

MATTI: I'm sorry I don't think I heard that properly.

JOHN: I was just a kid the first time I heard about you, Matti. Matti Aikio, a Sami author. We Sami had an author and one who was even respected in the capital. But now I don't quite know what to think of you. You have no self-respect!

MATTI: What has that to do with our financial arrangements?

JOHN: It has nothing to do with our "financial arrangements." I'm talking about your books.

MATTI: Have you read many of them?

JOHN: I've read all of them. But I didn't like your first two books, *Dressed in Animal Hide* and *Ginungagap*. They read as if they were written by a Norwegian. *The Son of a Hebrew,* on the other hand, was a really good book.

MATTI: *The Son of a Hebrew,* a book I wrote fifteen years ago when I happened to be preoccupied with the Jews?

JOHN: Fine, so let's say that it was about the Jews. At least that was what the Norwegian critics got out of it. But I saw much more in it, something which is of great importance to both of us—as artists and as Sami.

MATTI: (*Doesn't answer.*)

JOHN: (*Takes out* The Son of a Hebrew.) David Hesmon, who is the protagonist of your book, made a statue of Christ with Jewish features but he didn't dare exhibit it because he lived among Christians, quote: "He removed the Jewish features and remade the statue in the image of a white Christ." But the critics were savage and David was finished as an artist. He grew restless. Many years later he moved to Poland where his family lived. There he created a new statue of Christ but this time he didn't change it. "Christ, the Jew, stood there in front of him. One night his studio burned to the ground. The fire, however, did not manage to destroy his Christ. It had, rather, hardened it." Doesn't this reflect something you yourself have thought about and felt—that if you want to create something you must create out of your own experience? In other words, that Sami artists must create their art out of the spirit of the Sami?

MATTI: What are you talking about?

JOHN: Ráhkis ustit! [Dear Friend!] Don't you even understand Norwegian? It's no use speaking Norwegian or Sami to you. David Hesmon had the courage to gain his self-respect, but you don't. You just heap dirt on the coastal Sami and the southern Sami . . . Why? (*He begins to cough.*)

MATTI: Please continue your very capable presentation of David Hesmon's accomplishments. Maybe I should read you what happened after the Christian majority realized that it wasn't their Christ who had been resurrected from the burning ruins—it was a Jewish Christ. (*He reads.*) "Somewhere an inflammatory word was heard. The windows of the Jewish stores were smashed and an uncontrollable fury was suddenly sparked in the crowd. The sabres of the Cossacks were gleaming in the air. Screams of death were heard from the houses and in the streets. The monster raised its head and snarled, showing its teeth. . . . The vodka stands were attacked and barrels full of schnapps rolled into the streets. The monster roared and blood flowed into the gutter. Flames shot out from the Jewish quarter. The air was filled with the screams of death, and the Cossacks who dragged out from the bowels of the earth on this day rode through the street hollering in a drunken stupor. In the clear light of day women were raped. Those who escaped were tracked down on the tundra and by the river and were raped to the roaring laughter of the crowd. Others tracked the women like bloodhounds and chased them out of their hiding places. The monster and the spirit of the earth exulted in their celebratory orgy." Do you believe, John, that if David Hesmon had realized the consequences that he would have made such an image of Christ? I'm not so sure—even if you are.

JOHN: That wouldn't happen here. A pogrom? A massacre? Here in Norway? That's insane!

MATTI: You're young and naive, John. You've listened too closely to such political dreamers as Egede-Nissen, Ellisif Wessel, and Isak Saba. Don't you think that their peculiar blend of socialism and the cause of the Lapps could be quite inflammatory?

JOHN: Inflammatory?

MATTI: They speak out against the Norwegianization of the Lapps, against the boarding schools, against the military, against the business people . . .

JOHN: And against oppression. The fight against poverty and desperation in the Finnmark, and they know what they are talking about.

MATTI: Don't you see that they're Bolsheviks? They will give away our country to the Russian Bolsheviks . . .

JOHN: Nonsense!

MATTI: . . . those barbarians who believe that you can win by destroying everything. Do we have to leave the fate of humanity to the most unrefined instincts? Who, in any event, can guarantee that our current social conditions—as horrendous as they are—can be improved by one, or by five hundred revolutions? Ha, if a revolution is needed it will come all by itself. Nature will do what it always does—it will select the proper spirits to improve things. Lenin and Trotsky are not such spirits—they are demagogues!

JOHN: No, Lenin and Trotsky are not spirits. They are human beings and they will create a society where people are valued and not the spirits. The socialists, or the Bolsheviks as they call themselves in Russia, will struggle for a society where there is no exploitation, where those who create the wealth will control it.

MATTI: You must be aware that the Norwegian authorities are following very closely those kinds of orientations toward the east—and they will not treat deserters with kid gloves. We live in historical circumstances in which we cannot afford to provoke the Norwegian state. If we are to save what's left of the Sami culture we must assure the authorities that the Sami have nothing to do with the Bolsheviks, that, in fact, they are loyal citizens.

JOHN: Do you mean to say that in order to be Sami you have to be Norwegian?

MATTI: Rather that than Russian.

JOHN: Couldn't we just be ourselves?

MATTI: We have to be realistic. We have to think strategically.

JOHN: And according to your strategy we'd choose the European way?

MATTI: We live in Europe. They build our roads and our factories. They stand for progress. Why shouldn't we follow them?

JOHN: I see, So, it was as a European that you spoke at the first Sami congress in Trondheim! You said there that the coastal Sami are a backwards people who have ruined their property in drink and fled to the coast. That's not so! The coastal Sami have been around since the beginning of time. They were even involved in whaling and boat building before the Norwegians arrived with their explosive harpoons and eradicated the whales. And as to the southern Sami. Don't you realize what problems the new laws on reindeer breeding have created for them? The authorities have done everything to take away their pastures and use them for their own purposes. And they are trying to take away our language, so we can more easily be used as their slaves. That's why the Sami got together in Trondheim—while you sat in a restaurant slinging mud at the people leading the meeting. Why did you do that?

MATTI: What's wrong about sitting in a restaurant? You wouldn't have been able to sit through their prayer meetings either. Singing psalms, congratulating themselves, sending telegrams of praise to kings and prime ministers. Confused sentimental talk, hysterical agendas which didn't focus on anything. The only bright moment was Somby from Karasjok.

JOHN: (*Sarcastically*) Karasjok . . .

MATTI: He came forward quietly and in a crystal clear speech he told the saga of the moral conditions of the Lapps. He didn't talk about oppression, but about how the pastures could be divided and about how practical laws would limit the theft of reindeer. He spoke like an elder on law and public morality.

JOHN: Please, I read your so-called account of the events in your article. And you finish off your tribute to Somby by attributing his fine performance to his mixed noble Scandinavian blood, noting that the interior Finnmark is teeming with people like Somby. While the coastal Sami who have not been fortified by such blood, on the other hand, are a people of very limited intelligence and potential. Such a lie!

MATTI: Don't you think that the coastal Sami and the southern Sami are far gone? If we were to save Sami culture we will have to save it where it is possible, in the interior Finnmark!

JOHN: My God! People who truly have become more European than the Europeans themselves and who even refuse to speak Sami with their brothers should not be allowed to speak out on Sami matters. Stay here and continue to please the people you love so dearly. But do not speak on Sami issues, for you have no right to! (*He begins to exit.*)

MATTI: Jovna—vuordes veahas!

JOHN: (*He stops, his back to Matti.*)

MATTI: Do me a favor. Paint a picture about freedom.

JOHN: Freedom?

MATTI: I've seen that picture myself. . . . Two wild swans on a lake . . . sitting a little apart from each other . . . they're looking in opposite directions . . . The wind makes ripples in the surface . . . That is the most beautiful image of freedom I've ever seen in my life.

JOHN: And why do you want me to . . .

MATTI: You're the only one who could. Then I'll write the story of gesat.

JOHN: Gesat? Why?

MATTI: I'm actually working on a novel set in Karasjok called *Citizens and Nomads* but I'm not sure I'm able to write it. I haven't been up there in such a long time. So, I was thinking that perhaps I should write the story of a gesat instead.

JOHN: Why write a story about a reindeer calf who grows up among people and becomes domesticated?

MATTI: Gesat can never return to its herd. It would never survive. It also will never really become a domesticated animal like a cow or a goat, but it still has its own worth. Life is good to gesat. But, then, one day it does something it never should have done. It gores a human. And it is butchered.

JOHN: And?

MATTI: No, it's probably a little banal, but I began to think that perhaps I've become such a gesat. I've been here thirty years now and I've become part of my environment. But people don't feel comfortable with me anyway. Just as I'm not comfortable with them. So they watch me and think . . . when will he begin butting with his head? They keep an eye on what I write. Is his Norwegian any good? Does he write things which are appropriate? Is it morally good? Is it refined? What does Aikio say on Sami issues? Is he one of those bolsheviks? How does Aikio relate to Norwegian interests? You're lucky to be a painter. They won't turn your every line inside out—which they do to every single word I write.

JOHN: And, naturally, you pay attention to that?

MATTI: Yes, I do but not solely because of the private reasons you have in mind, but because I'm an intellectual. Because I'm the only intellectual Sami in Oslo I've been elevated to some kind of authority on Sami matters. I've been given the job of a political high wire act—a job I never asked for. All I wanted was to become a writer . . . a free and unencumbered spirit. But they have caught me. I eat out of their hands and I sleep in their house. But what will happen the day gesat butts his head? (*He looks at John, who doesn't respond.*) That's all. Good-bye.

JOHN: You almost put me in a sentimental mood, Matti, but your story about gesat doesn't quite work. I have never heard of a gesat who attacks his herd the way you do. Gesat doesn't like the herd, and the herd doesn't care for gesat. (*He is about to leave.*)

MATTI: (*He opens his manuscript and begins to burn it.*)

JOHN: What are you doing?

MATTI: The herd should not care about gesat.

JOHN: All that talk about gesat was just nonsense. You are a human being—with a mind. You're not an animal driven by your instincts.

MATTI: A human being? With a mind? No, I'm an animal. (*He takes another page and begins to burn it.*)

JOHN: (*He tries to prevent him but then he begins to cough violently and faints.*)

Matti burns his manuscript: Sverre Porsanger and Nils Gaup. Photograph by
Ola Røe.

MATTI: John, what's the matter? I didn't know you were this ill. Can you
hear me? My God, what have I done? John, wake up—keep
fighting—for you and for me. John. Oh, my God. (*He kneels at
John's side. Then he gets up and sits by his desk. Suddenly he
senses another person in the room.*) Who are you?

DIEĐIHEADDJI: The one who brings knowledge.

MATTI: Knowledge . . . ? I must be dreaming.

DIEĐIHEADDJI: A dream that's real.

MATTI: Where did you come from?

Matti encounters Dieðiheaddji: Knut Walle and Nils Gaup. Photograph by
Ola Røe.

DIEÐIHEADDJI: I come from the other place.

MATTI: Why are you here?

DIEÐIHEADDJI: I come to see the sick in his hour of need.

MATTI: Have you come for John? But he is so young . . . there's still so
    much for him to do . . .

DIEÐIHEADDJI: No.

MATTI: You've come for me then? But I'm not ill.

DIEÐIHEADDJI: You have many wounds, so many that you won't survive them.

MATTI: But there's so much to do . . . I don't understand.

DIEÐIHEADDJI: No one understands. You'll have to write again the two pages you threw in the fire. Of all your mistakes this was the biggest. You've worn out your life to be able to write that book. It is an important part of the achievements of our people. It cannot burn.

MATTI: But will anyone value it?

DIEÐIHEADDJI: I said so.

MATTI: But my other books—what about them?

DIEÐIHEADDJI: Maybe.

MATTI: So everything has been in vain.

DIEÐIHEADDJI: No. It's been necessary. Write. I'll be back again and then you'll have to come with me.

MATTI: Just one more question. What will happen to the Sami? Will we survive?

DIEÐIHEADDJI: European culture has drawn a battle line. Its future does not look bright. The Europeans are trying to subjugate Nature. They will destroy themselves in the attempt. Good-bye.

JOHN: (*Coughs.*)

MATTI: (*Wakes up as if from a trance.*) John!

JOHN: It's not dangerous. It's worst during the winter.

MATTI: I've had the same thing but I got rid of it when I was young.

People took care of me. You must make sure that you're not cold. You must eat well. You'll have to go north.

JOHN: I wish people would pay more for my paintings even if they don't understand the struggle behind each of them.

MATTI: Listen, John. I have achieved a certain position as a writer. Perhaps I could ask a few of my more well known colleagues to give you some good references to those who award grants, then we could . . . (*There's a knock on the door.*) Come in!

THE HOTEL MGR: May I interrupt for a moment?

MATTI: (*Makes a friendly gesture.*)

THE HOTEL MGR: I've received a letter from Aschehoug Publishers. Would you please take a look at it?

MATTI: (*Reads the letter and says while reading:*) I see. They've sent my advance directly to the hotel again.

THE HOTEL MGR: I think they prefer it that way.

MATTI: And the amount covers next week's rent as well.

THE HOTEL MGR: That's correct. (*He goes to the door.*)

MATTI: Dear sir. I would like to make a request. This young man is a very talented artist from the Finnmark. He is on his way up there to find inspiration for his paintings. But he is in need of funds for his journey. If you would give me the amount for next week's rent we would be able to help him on his way. I will, naturally, produce an equal sum by tomorrow afternoon at five. If not, I'm ready to pack my suitcases and move into the nearest snowdrift.

THE HOTEL MGR: You're certain you're not just involving yourself in a new set of problems . . . Oh well, it's your money after all . . . In that case I'd ask the young . . . publisher to my office.

MATTI: Thank you very much. I was certain you'd understand.

JOHN: I'm fine. I'll be all right. You're the one who needs peace to work . . .

MATTI: Go to the office and get the money. I've done this sort of thing for thirty years, so I'll be fine.

JOHN: Thank you, Matti.

MATTI: Good-bye, my young friend. Remember that you have a large task ahead of you.

JOHN: (*In the doorway*) Do you think people will ever take our work seriously?

MATTI: A time will come when the light will be softer and not hurt the eyes so much.

JOHN: Good-bye. (*He exits.*)

MATTI: (*Picks up a pen and begins to write:*) Dear Mr. Nygaard. For several good reasons I would like you to consider the possibility of Aschehoug and Co. publishing a new and improved edition of my book *Letters from the Polar Circle* this spring. I am making this suggestion because I see no other way of acquiring the necessary funds for me to get out of town to finish my novel of the Finnmark, *Citizens and Nomads*. I am quite convinced that, given the proper peace and quiet to work in, I would be able to write a fairly important novel. On the other hand, should I be unable to get out of my current situation, I run the risk of abandoning the book only half completed.

(*A text appears on the screen:*
Matti Aikio was never to see the novel published. He died that same year, 1929. The novel was published shortly after his death, entitled *The Settlement at the Riverbank*.)

THE STUDENT: So ends the story of two Sami artists from the beginning of the century that we are now on our way out of. Our only consolation is that it happened back then and not today. This can give us hope.

The End

Homecoming

An Alaskan Native's Quest
for Self-Esteem

Written by Joshua Weiser
Co-directed by Joshua Weiser
and John Pingayak

Characters

PINGI: The voice of wisdom and translator for the Elder.

THE ELDER: Counsels "Troubled Youth" through conveyance of traditional values.

TROUBLED YOUTH (or Sammy): Represents the dilemma faced by many present-day native Americans.

FOUR DRIFTWOODS: Convey traditional values related to a subsistence life-style.

JUNIOR: The second voice of wisdom and translator for the Elder.

TWO "STORY-KNIVES": Storytellers who use the traditional story-knife.

AUDIENCE FACILITATORS: (Maxine, Allen, Don, Shawn, Valeria, Jennifer) Motivate audience into interaction.

Note: All cast members double as Cup'ik dancers.

1: Entrance Song/Dance: "Yuggeuma"

*(Cast dances toward stage singing.
Begin background drum as Pingi, "The voice of wisdom," looks
at driftwood. Finding one he likes, he holds it up, praising the
wood's quality in Cup'ik. Then, looking at audience, he says:)*

PINGI: Our land has always provided for our people. Like her children,
we treat her with love and respect. And her gifts are many! The
Ocean gives us the seal and walrus. Our rivers and streams give
us the salmon, the pike, chee, black and needle fish. The skies
give us winged creatures. The land gives us furs to keep us warm
and sweet black, blue, and salmon berries. Even the little mouse
helps us by collecting sweet roots.

But our greatest gift, born in the land of trees and delivered to us
on the Kuskoquim and Yukon River highway, is the driftwood.

This (holding up driftwood) is nature's gift from which our ancestors formed the tools that have carried on our traditions to this very
day.

This gives us a way to share our joys and to pay respect to the
Great Spirit that dwells within the sea, the sky, and the land.

To understand more fully, let us go to the edge of the Bering Sea
where driftwoods are gently bobbing in the ocean current.

(Looks out onto the sea; spots driftwood and says:)

Aah! There they are! Now listen, listen closely, and you'll hear
them speak of their futures.

2. Driftwoods Speak

(Begin arctic wilderness soundtrack.)

DRIFTWOOD #1: Say, neighbors, what's going to happen when we finally
get beached?

DRIFTWOOD #2: Someone's going to roll me over and see how good I am. Then they'll take me home and carve me into a harpoon.

DRIFTWOOD #3: I have brought back the mighty bearded seal. I have carried many a hunter through storm and calm. I will become a great Kayak and insure the survival of my people.

DRIFTWOOD #4: Not me, I was made to hold food. I'll be carved into ten beautiful bowls with artwork all over.

DRIFTWOOD #1: I'm going to be a strong bow and many swift arrows.

DRIFTWOOD #2: The spirits have blessed my wood; I'll be changed into masks that will praise the creatures of our land.

DRIFTWOOD #3: Skilled dancers will put you on their faces, and I will provide the rhythm that will move you through the air. I will be changed into a great symbol of peace, the dancing drum.

DRIFTWOOD #4: As my fibers are very strong, I will give shelter to the people of this land; I will be part of a great man's sod house.

DRIFTWOOD #1: All of you are missing the greatest fun of all. I'm going to snap, crackle, and pop! I'm going to burn baby burn and give warmth to all who come near.

3. Sammy Interrupts

SAMMY: And I'm going to take a hike because you guys are b o r i n g !

All this stuff about driftwood and your candy words about gifts from the land doesn't mean you-know-what to me.

Bows, arrows, harpoons, and dance masks . . . Man this is the twentieth century! Not Disneyland!

Hey, this is the age of green paper. If you got it, you're somebody. If you don't, you're on welfare; a nobody. (*pause*) And me, I'm on the big city streets looking for work 'cause there's nothing happening at home Nothing! I can't even find a good job 'cause I don't have a piece of paper that says I'm worth something.

You get what I'm saying? Nothing you're doing up there makes any sense . . . *To me!*

Why don't you tell these people how it really is . . . without trying to paint a rosy picture of native people?

JUNIOR: (Cup'ik) How is it, really?

SAMMY: Hey, English, man, English . . . I'm Eskimo all right but boarding schools and television took my language away, so *speak English.*

JUNIOR: How is it, really?

SAMMY: Hey, I'll tell you, man, I'm going to come on that stage and tell you, and you, and you, and . . . the whole world!

My wife just left me; left me flat! 'Cause I can't quit what my daddy's been doing ever since I learned to crawl, *Drinking!*

You see here a man who's been hurting from day one (*pointing to himself*). But do you know what that hurt is? I see all these fancy-dressed people out there and I wonder, do you know or even care why a guy like me walks the streets with a time bomb inside of him?
(*Sammy pauses, retreating deep within himself; Junior walks over putting an arm on his shoulder. Sammy pushes his arm away and, looking right at him, says:*)

SAMMY: I don't know how to talk to you; *I don't know how to talk to you, because . . . my . . . my . . .*

JUNIOR: Parents . . .

SAMMY: My folks never talked to me, never spoke to me in Cup'ik, never taught me how to live, never . . .

JUNIOR: Cared?

SAMMY: (*Nodding*)

Did they ever *once* ask, "How was your day?" "Is everything all right?" "Do you need anything?"

They didn't have the time. They were too busy making home brew, arguing, and beating up each other. And when they're straight, mom's blowing our welfare bucks on bingo six nights a week and dad's glued to the TV.

(*Walks over to students*)

And us kids, we don't have time either. We're too busy trying to escape the pain of living at home; trying to find, in the middle of the night, a warm place to sleep and something to eat. We're too busy trying to have a "good time." (*pause*) But what's there to do?

Today, we live in our villages with our fancy snowmachines and three-wheelers, and we're all too busy living our separate lives . . . too busy to talk, to listen, to . . . care.

(*As if waking up from a dream*)

And you're dancing around on stage with logs on your backs. Hey, what am I doing telling my life story to all these strangers . . . Hey, I'm gone!

4. Sammy's Healing Begins

(*Sammy walks away; Junior calls to him. Sammy stops and listens as Junior translates.*)

JUNIOR: He wants you, (*pause for name*) . . .

SAMMY: Pee Wee Herman . . .

JUNIOR: Come on, what's your real name?

SAMMY: Sammy.

JUNIOR: Sammy, he wants you to come talk to him. (*Jumps off stage and brings him to the Elder.*)
(*Junior and Pingi have a heated moment of Cup'ik discussion with the Elder, explaining to him the essence of what Sammy told the audience.*)

JUNIOR: (*translates for the Elder*)
I hear your words. I feel your pain, your anger, your confusion. And I congratulate you. You've shown the courage to open your heart to all of us and to let your spirit ask for help. Tell me, Sammy, have you ever experienced any kind of success in your life? (*No response.*) Would it be true to say that you don't think too much of yourself?

SAMMY: (*Responds with a nod.*)

JUNIOR: (*Translates:*) You've started your healing by taking a risk and being honest.

When a man does not take care of his spirit, he gets used to failing. Elders advise him, but he's so lost within himself that he hears nothing except his own problems, and spends his life running away from himself.

We're going to heal your spirit in our Cup'ik way and give you a taste of real success.
(*Pingi assembles all into dancing positions.*)

SAMMY: Oh no you don't! I'm no Eskimo dancer! You're not going to make a fool out of me in front of all these people! (*Gets up to leave.*)

JUNIOR: See! You've failed already and you haven't even tried! Please, Sammy!

5. Sammy's Pancake Dance

(*Sammy tries to give up twice but is encouraged by the group to continue. He shows great improvement as the beat enters him and pushes out all negative thoughts.*)

6. Sammy is dressed in Cup'ik Clothes

(*After the dance, all clap, gather around Sammy and show their joy over his new-found success. They dress him in traditional Cup'ik clothes. A pair of "clean" underwear is pulled from his pants and thrown into the audience.*)

JUNIOR: (*motioning to his heart*) How do you feel now?

SAMMY: Better than I have in a looonng time! I feel like . . . jumping for joy!

7. Blanket Toss

(*Allen pulls Sammy aside and motions for the group to huddle, explaining the blanket toss. All excitedly agree, get blanket, and toss Sammy three times.*)

8. Elder Engages Sammy in Drumming

EARL: (*Translates:*) He wants you to sit by him and help him drum so we can burn a hole in the floor doing a dance in your honor!

9. Sammy's Honor Dance

(*Celebrating his return to himself.*)

10. The Spiritual Meaning of Eskimo Dance

(*Pingi tells all to sit down.*)

PINGI: You are a great dancer, Sammy. All of you are. But where did

those movements come from? What goes on in the mind of a
person who creates an Eskimo dance? Do any of you know?

MAXINE: You've got to *feel something?*

PINGI: Exactly! You've got to be humble enough to see it in your mind,
to smell it, taste it, and *feel it;* to feel the rhythm in all of nature.
It's like your story-knife!

11. Story-knife Scene
Maxine and Jennifer

PINGI: Beautiful! There was rhythm in your story! The way you spit and
how your voice went up and down. Your mind was so strong that
you brought the story to life! Right? (*All laugh with understanding.*)

And the driftwood has given us a special gift; (*grabs drum*) with
this, we can create the rhythm of life anytime we wish. This is
our heartbeat.

(*Begins drum*)

Before our people understood this special gift, there were constant
wars. Conflict between tribes was resolved with bow, arrows, and
all kinds of death.

Then the day came when we realized that our problems could be
resolved without one drop of blood being shed. We could dance
away our frustrations, in bad times and the good times.

We realized that dances could express the joy of living and turn
dark mid-winter days into a warm spring day on the tundra. The
wind is gently blowing through the grass, making a swish sound,
making your tent flutter. The sky is full of cackling birds. The
ocean spray gently touches your face. Fish jump out of the water.
On a nearby ice floe, a group of seals are tanning in the midday
sun unaware that a hunter is quietly approaching them by Kayak
(Te-cum-te-cum).

JUNIOR: Like that salmonberry dance!

12. Junior describes Salmonberry Dance

JUNIOR: You go out looking for yummy berries (*motions for drum rhythm*), you find a beautiful patch. You pick some, throw one up into the air and . . . (*sound*) Delicious!
(*All pick up rhythm of speech, get into it. Junior starts working with audience.*

JUNIOR: Pick another one, look this way, that way . . . (*sound*)

13. You Are Never Alone, Sammy

(*Group's joy suddenly stops as Sammy moves forward in sudden depression. Junior and Pingi look at each other, then approach Sammy.*)

SAMMY: What happens . . . What happens when you guys go? I'll be alone again.

PINGI: You are not alone with the feelings you have. Look out there, Sammy. What do you see? There is our great human family which you are a part of. All of them know what you're going through because, in one way or other, they've been there.

JUNIOR: (*Putting arm around Sammy*) Now look at this man's smiling face . . . Look at it! In less than thirty minutes, you've changed from thinking of yourself as being no better than a moldy piece of dry fish, to a true Nukalpiat, a man in his prime with all the confidence he needs to accomplish anything he chooses.

PINGI: Today, Sammy has begun to journey back to himself, rediscovering the personal worth he lost as a child. One day he will return to his village and be a great inspiration to his people.

And the same is true for that traditional council member, that city council member, that teacher, that health aide, and that school board member, and these student council members!

As each of us begins to take care of our inner spirit and *really communicate* with each other, our communities will again become positive and strong, glowing with mutual respect.

14. Audience Shakes Hands

(*Student led by Leo gets idea and quickly voices it in Cup'ik to Senior, John, and the Elder. With approval, they proceed.*)

LEO: We did something at a youth leadership conference that we want to share with all of you.

JENNIFER: Before we do our "One People Dance," let's all show each other how beautiful we all are. Everyone stand up! Look at the beautiful people on your right; now, your other side.

DON: Now look at the beautiful people on your left.

VALERIA: Look at the handsome men in front of you.

SHAWN: Now look at the gorgeous women in back of you.

JENNIFER: Now move around and get people's names, hotel room numbers, and shake at least ten hands. Go!

15. Sammy Thanks Audience

SAMMY: (*To audience*) Hey, I just want to thank all of you for coming here and helping me out; you're all beautiful, really! And you know what? (*pause*) So Am I!

16. One People Quyana Dance

17. Encore: Jump Rope Song

The End

III

Interviews

The Birth of the Tũkak' Theater

An Interview with
Reidar Nilsson, Artistic Director

Per Brask

(From conversations between Reidar Nilsson and Per Brask in Toronto, April 15 and 16, 1989. Translated from the Danish by the interviewer.)

How did a Norwegian actor get started making theater in Denmark with a group of Inuit from Greenland?

Out of furious anger. Anger and a meaningful coincidence. I was "imported" as an actor into Denmark in 1972 by the Odin Teatret in Holstebro. And once I was invited to dinner at the Greenlander House in that city. I fell in love with the woman who was running the House, Elin, and I ended up living there. In my spare time away from the Odin Teatret I would be working around the house, and one day Elin said: "Create a show or some kind of event for the fifth anniversary of the House." Which I then did, and out of that three things happened. First, an old woman of about seventy who hadn't spoken to me in the two years I'd stayed at the Greenlander House said: "You must take this performance to Sukkertop-pen [in Greenland]." She was born there. So I asked her, "How do you think they'd react to seeing this show?" Because this show wasn't native theater. It was based on the legend of how humans were given the sacred gift of feasting. So, she answered: "First they'll laugh. Then they'll grow silent. And then it will become dangerous to be a Dane in Greenland." Secondly, the day after the opening of the show I drove a Greenlandic politician to the airport. He was one of the young radicals who'd participated in occupying the Ministry of Greenland in Copenhagen to protest the oil exploration around Greenland. Remember this was in the early seventies, before the commission studying the possibilities of Home Rule for Greenland had been appointed. He was usually very talkative but in the car he was very quiet, so I asked him: "What's the matter?" "I'm thinking about the performance I saw yesterday," he said, "I've always been very aggressive, politically, and I've always felt that all the romantic talk about being a Greenlander is useless. During the show I felt tears welling up in my eyes and I tried to get into a position where no one else would be able to see me cry. But when I turned around I noticed that other people were crying also; I wasn't alone with my tears, so I let them fall. You must make more theater like that." Thirdly, some of the people who were in the show said to me: "We have always wanted to become actors, and we have applied to the various theatre schools but we are often told that Hamlet wasn't written for a bow-legged man with slanted eyes and black hair." No admittance to these people who are Danish citizens! So I bought myself a plane ticket and went to Copenhagen, where I went to Niels Mathiassen's [then Denmark's Social Democratic minister of culture] office. I didn't have an appointment but I told his staff that I'd stay until he had time to see me. Finally, he could see me and I told him this very story and I ended up saying: "Minister, that's completely unacceptable." And he said: "You're right. Why don't you set up a theatre school for Greenlanders?" So, I ended up making Inuit theater because I fell in love with a woman cooking a huge meal at the Greenlander House.

After this meeting how did Tūkak' come into existence?
Well, after this we received some funding from the Kaj Munk Fund, the pools, and from the Nordic Council. Then things could happen. And a year and half later we were able to move to the farm at Fjaltring. But for the first year and a half we worked in the dining room at Holstebro. Three times a day we had to rearrange the space back into a dining room.

How many actors were involved at that time?
Well, not yet actors. But there were five people who wanted to make theater and myself.

Tell me about the relationship between yourself, a Norwegian, and five Inuit in the process of making native theater.

I only know that if I had been a Dane it wouldn't have worked. I think that it was important that I was an artist they knew, an artist who worked in that city. I also had the right kind of temperament. We lived in the same house and ate the same food. In addition, my roots were in Norse mythology; I wasn't a Christian missionary. And, we had had a lot of discussions about myths and legends, and we had told each other lots of stories in the time that we had lived in the same house. So, we had established a closeness. All five of the people had a desire to create, an artistic need, though only two of them knew that they wanted to be actors. And they all felt a need to do something for their country, and to do it artistically. They all had a need to get something out of their bodies. It was a truly exciting time with discussions and demonstrations. This was around the same time that the negotiations about Home Rule began, in 1975. So, the main focus of our work was the question of identity. What does it mean to be Danish? What does it mean to be a Greenlander? The majority of people in Greenland are of mixed background. Many of them are blond and have eyes bluer than mine, the result of four hundred years of colonization and intermingling on the west coast. So, the question of identity became in intriguing one. When we gave our group a name we had to think about these things, because the naming of your children is a very important, very responsible task. First of all, what is the word for theater in Greenlandic? Well, it doesn't exist. There is no direct translation. That was our first task, defining what we meant by theater. What is theater? But we found a different word, a long word which means "a group of people who are working on something which they'd like to communicate to other people and share it with them," which is the perfect description of what theater does. The word *Tūkak'* [harpoon tip] we chose because we were in the middle of a political conflict.

What is Inuit Theater, as opposed to any other kind of theater?

In this context I intensely dislike the word *native*. I think it causes so many misunderstandings. My family has lived in the same place in Norway since the year 700. Am I "native" or not? Why should I have to justify myself and my work like so many whites who work in what's called "native" theater feel they have to? When we started we were asked to create our theater in Greenland, and I said "I don't want to live in

Greenland." Because I know that in Greenland I will be seen as a guest. So, I said: "If you want to make theater with me then come here." You see, I don't train Inuit, Indian, Sami, that is native, actors. I train *actors*. Nobody calls me a Norwegian actor; I'm an actor who happens to have been born in Norway. I made movies in Paris; no one talked about me as a Norwegian actor. I was an actor. That's the difference. And that's why it's been so difficult and taken so long to get that kind of theater going here in North America in a strong and powerful manner. The emphasis has been wrong. Now Tomson Highway is succeeding in Canada because he knows that the key to making it work is artistic; naturally political issues are involved, but the foundation is the artist. To become a good artist, and not to be admired as a novelty. I have insisted on that from the beginning.

Tell me about the basis of your artistry, about why you as an artist became involved in this way.

I hold a profound belief, which is that every single person on the earth is beautiful. We have all been born with a sun shining inside us, a source of life. We may have been born into different backgrounds, but we've all got a sun inside, a will to life. So when I wanted to realize my sense of the theater I knew that it had to focus on desire for life, light, and hope. And that's what I've devoted my life to. Because no matter how horrible things get in this world, there is hope, there is life. That's the drive, that's the engine behind every show we create. These individual desires for life, these different suns are, of course, also the source of conflict and drama. I mean if we all went around nodding our heads in agreement all the time we'd lose our teeth, we'd be incapacitated. We must stay on the edge, we must make theater dangerous. Let me tell you a story. I think it's a Chinese story. There once were four moths who were sitting around talking about life and light. They had a kind of debating club for moths. Naturally they couldn't agree on anything. One night one of them sees a light. He approaches it but returns quickly to tell the others about it, describing it as cool and blue. The others don't believe him. The next night another of them sees the light, and thinks "I guess he was right then. There is a light over there." So he moves closer to it. When he returns he says, "You're right that there was a light over there, but it isn't cool, it's warm and yellow." So, the two of them got into a fight. The other two shook their heads. The third night, the third moth sees the light and flies toward it. "The first moth was right, it is cool. No, no, the second one was right too, it's getting warmer." So, he became really curious and got so close that he singed one of his wings. "Ouch! That hurt." So, when he returned to the others he told them about it and said, "Here's my proof, just look! You two just talk, I came back with proof." The next night the fourth moth ventures out, and he too registers what the others have talked about the closer he gets. But he stays in the flame, where he burns up, becoming the light. You see, if you don't want to become the light then forget about the theater. That's what we're aiming for at the Tūkak'.

Next story, please.

In 1972 or '73 we had a seminar on Kathakali theater and Balinese dance, and a lot of groups and individuals showed up. There I met a flautist from India; he was a history professor at a university there. He was playing his flute and he was incredible. So I asked him, "It must be fantastic to be one of the world's finest flautists?" He stood up and looked at me. "Poor little boy," he said, "poor little boy, let me tell you a little story. A long time ago India was made up of many different kingdoms and in one of those kingdoms there was a very sad king. Nobody could cheer him up; all his advisers and viziers tried to no avail. They brought in belly dancers, clowns, and entertainers of all kinds, but nothing worked. The king stayed very sad. So, one of the king's adviser's thought: "We haven't tried music, yet. Maybe we should bring in the finest musician in the kingdom." He happened to be a flautist and he was brought to the court where he played for the king, who became happy. So the king said: "You who are the finest musician in my kingdom, you can have whatever you desire." The flautist answered: "My dear little king, come along with me." And they went down to the beach where the flautist pointed out at the sea: "What is that?" he asked. "Well, it's the sea," the king said. Then the flautist bent down and cupped his hands, filling them with water which dripped out between his fingers. "What are those?" he asked the king. "Those are water drops," the king answered. "My music is like drops in the ocean of music," the flautist said." That story put me in my place. That story told me that the artistic pursuit is not a question of being the best there is, it is a pursuit of honesty, a question of being genuine. To be seeking. Being known, fame, must not interfere with the work because that will make it dishonest.

Your stories are producing some echoes in my mind. Right now the name I hear is Artaud.

(Laughter.) The inspiration is naturally Artaud's Balinese dream. I haven't seen any of Artaud's theater work, who has? But what he was striving for and the manner in which he described his experience of Balinese dance at the World Exhibition in 1926 we can learn from and find inspiration in. But where he sought experiences through the use of drugs, I must be completely clear-headed when I create. The work must be precise.

Let's return to the development of the Tūkak' Teatret.
Well, initially the intention was that I was to work with the group for sixteen months and then they would go back to Greenland to work. So, the beginning was intended as a sixteen-month experiment. But as we were working along on the issues of identity it occurred to each of the five people that they wanted to return to their respective areas of Greenland; they weren't going to settle in the same place. They wanted to start their own groups in separate places, which is incredibly difficult, of course. So, we extended the sixteen months to five years and for that we needed a place to work in peace and quiet. We knew that we wanted to find a place by the ocean. In Greenland everyone lives by the ocean, and I came from the mountains of Norway, so we were all missing the power of the elements in the rolling hills of Denmark. In fact, every weekend we would leave Holstebro and go to Fjaltring [a village by the North Sea, where the Tūkak' theater is now located] to spend time by the ocean. So we knew that we wanted to find a farm by the North Sea to work in. We took trips from the furthest south to the furthest north until finally we found an empty farm in Fjaltring which had been expropriated by the state. After a meeting with the farmers of the committee who decided whether we could move in, we took over three farms in the area and began to renovate.

How was the play Inuit *developed?*
Originally I wrote the script that became *Inuit* for a completely different show when I'd just moved to Denmark. It was a script trying to come to terms with some of Jung's theories of individuation in the "clothing" of Norse mythology. So I suggested that we adapt that script dressing it in Inuit "clothing." The whole idea of dealing with individuation in the context of our discussion around identity made a lot of sense. So, first we looked at the script in the context of forty or fifty Greenlandic myths and stories. And soon we found the connection between Norse and Green-

landic myths, and then we found the right characters in Greenlandic mythology. The whole process took us about a year. It was an exciting time. Each day someone would have the task of finding a myth or legend to tell and that day we would do our practical work around that story. That way we build up a powerful library of stories. That is how *Inuit* evolved, through continual improvisations around stories. That show is now twelve years old and we've performed it maybe two or three thousand times now, all over Denmark, Scandinavia, many different cities in Europe, twenty two in the United States, Canada; almost every village in Alaska has seen it, Costa Rica, etc., etc.

How did the audiences in Greenland respond to Inuit?

Incredibly well. Incredibly well. Remember that *Inuit* is a very contemporary theater piece; it is not a traditional theater piece. In Greenland they almost pronounced it a national play. They thought it was an enactment of a Greenlandic myth. All the reactions we got were very strong and not just positive; some reacted very negatively. For example, some people felt that the show was sacreligious because of a scene that is structured liturgically. We used elements of the Catholic mass as a symbol of forces from the outside, imperialism, forces which repress a culture. In Holsteinsborg I was called to a meeting with the minister there. He flung biblical quotations at me to show how evil I'd been in bringing the show to Greenland. However, I know the Bible quite well so I could answer him back with different quotes. He was furious and afraid. The next day the whole group of us were invited to meet with his Greenlandic colleague, who loaded us with gifts in gratitude for having brought what he felt was the most Christian performance he'd ever seen, a show which reflected his own personal development. An old woman came up to me the day after we had performed on the Faeroe Islands and told me off because the show had made her realize that her relationship with her husband was built on a lie and now she had to leave him. You see, *Inuit* doesn't address a particular issue for the mind, it aims at your heart and your guts because it talks about human beings in their process of life. The first minister I told you about left Greenland about half a year later to join the Grey Brothers in Newfoundland. When we were in Canada the next year we were prevented by a storm from performing in his community, but when we came back to Denmark I read in a Christian newspaper he sent columns to that I was a leader of "neo-hedonism, if not satanism." This column led to a two-month-long war of letters to the editor. When theater can effect those kinds of reactions at least you know your work isn't toothless. I think *Inuit* is able to touch people like that because it doesn't give answers, it doesn't tell people how to live. The political theater of the sixties and seventies attempted to achieve that kind of reaction, but because theaters tried to tell people how to live and think, which is really just another form of imperialism, they couldn't do it. *Inuit* is also a simple show and it concerns something simple, namely pride in who you are no matter who you are. It demands nothing of you but it makes you ask questions about yourself. Externally, it talks about cultural imperialism, about how the white spirit forces masks on people. But the internal story is about the necessity of struggle, not against things but struggle with what happens in your life.

What language(s) do you perform it in?
Our current production is in Greenlandic. We've played it in Danish, in English, in Italian.

How does the language affect the show?
It depends on the composition of the cast. We played it with an international cast in English. But when we play with an Inuit cast we play in Greenlandic. And, when we're performing in Paris, for example, the audience naturally doesn't understand the dialogue. But they are then forced to listen to the sounds of a language they don't understand and it turns into music, to poetry. It's a very beautiful show that way because it totally becomes evident.

What was the next phase in Tūkak's development?
The first conference of the ICC [the Inuit Circumpolar Conference, a political organization speaking on behalf of all Inuit] took place in 1978 in Alaska. *Inuit* was to be performed at the opening ceremonies. Now *Inuit* is a mask show, and the churches had outlawed the use of the mask in Alaska in the same way that they had outlawed the use of the drum in Greenland. So when we appeared in masks, it created quite an impact. The next morning the mayor had written a large sign saying that even if the ICC didn't make it as an organization the expense of the conference had been well justified by our performance. Strong words. At the conference there were observers from the World Council of Indigenous Peoples and they expressed a desire to create theater like ours. So we were asked to expand our composition. So we began to train Indians, Sami, and others

and for the next five years we were an indigenous peoples' theater. But as our basis as a theater had come out of our discussions about identity, we now had to start those considerations over again. What are we now? Our world had grown. We support minority rights. Why do we do that? What kind of theater do we want to make? This gave us new energy and new horizons. We could no longer navel gaze. Our work changed and we began working in English, though none of us were native to the English language. Our work centered increasingly around universal issues, as we no longer could work out of a specific cultural context. We became a new theater. We worked out of a sense of comparative mythology. At the end of this period we adapted George Ryga's *The Ecstasy of Rita Joe* into a show we called *Sinatoq/The Dream,* in which we had twenty two actors from twelve different countries. It opened in 1985 and it was our tenth-anniversary show. After having worked as an indigenous peoples' theater for a few years I began to grow restless and impatient. We are all affected by various forms of cultural imperialism. It became important for me to say and give expression to the fact that these issues are not confined to the indigenous peoples. *Sinatoq/The Dream* became an important show in telling people that we were more than an Inuit theater. Though there has been a theater in Greenland, Silamiut, since 1984, and Greenland achieved Home Rule in 1979 (responsibility for the areas of education and culture was transferred in 1980), we have been running a school partially funded by the Home Rule government. The school will finally move to Nuuk in 1992 because Greenland now has a cultural policy in place. Which I'm really looking forward to because I dislike schools, in particular schools of art. The past few years we've been working on an international Tûkak'. I've always been fascinated by William Blake and in order to do something that took us as far away as possible from so-called "native" theater we started to create a show around Blake's *The Marriage of Heaven and Hell,* which we called *For Hell's Sake.* The Danish novelist Jytte Borberg was involved in this show. Her novel *Masquerade* published in 1988 is the basis of the show we will begin to work on in September 1989 (and with which we will celebrate our fifteenth anniversary in 1990). *For Hell's Sake* proved conclusively that our company consisted of actors, not Inuit actors, Asian actors, Indian actors, or whatever. They are *actors.* We are ready for the next phase.

What do you want to do with Tûkak' now?
I want to live! I want life!

Performance in the Fourth World

An Interview with
Ulla Ryum

Per Brask

I am writing
in a foreign language
. . . .
on the page my words
become increasingly
blurred
they are pulled down into
the words below
as if
consumed
from beneath

> (From the poetry collection *Skrift* by the Sami writer Ailo Gaup.
> Translated from the Norwegian by P.B.)

Since her debut as a novelist in 1962, the Danish playwright and director Ulla Ryum has published four novels, three collections of short stories, and two collection of essays. She has had eleven plays produced, several radio plays, ballet scenarios, operas, and TV dramas. Many of these she has directed herself for different regional theaters in Denmark and at the Royal Theatre in Copenhagen. Her work is fueled by intense ecological concerns and by a meticulous analysis of human relationships.

The Danish playwright and dramaturg Ulla Ryum. Photograph by Gautam Dasgupta.

She has been extremely active in writers' organizations and involved in several governmental committees.

Ryum has also written extensively on dramaturgical theory. Her own dramaturgical model illustrates a nonlinear, non-Aristotelian approach toward the elucidation of a dramatic question. The process as Ryum outlines it allows for greater audience participation, in the sense that the audience is not being forced to accept the conditions upon which the story develops, but rather is encouraged to relate to possibilities, suggestions. A play then does not move toward resolution but aims at insight into the conditions activated by dramatic issues. It is from this sense of dramaturgical democracy that she conducts her intercultural work with the Sami and with Faeroe Islanders.

The Sami are an indigenous people living in the Polar region of Fennoscandia, inhabiting the northern parts of Norway, Sweden, Finland, and the Kola Peninsula in the Soviet Union. They have lived in these areas for over four thousand years. Only a small portion of Sami herd reindeer; many are involved in fishing (including whaling), farming, hunting, and other industries, depending on where they live. They have been exposed to many kinds of oppression from the countries in which they live—from being forcibly converted to Christianity to having their lands and their language taken away—a story not unfamiliar to many peoples of the Fourth World.

(From a conversation with Ulla Ryum at her home in Farum, Denmark in November 1988. Translated from the Danish by the interviewer.)

When did your first meeting with the Sami culture take place?

As a part of my hotel training—my training involved tourist hotels, resort hotels as opposed to business hotels in the cities. I apprenticed, starting in 1956, with the Swedish Tourist Association, which runs a number of hotels in Sweden. I was sent to a hotel in Ammarnäss, which is located in a part of Lapland. It was the first time I was that far north. Ammarnäss proved to be one of the most lively and still functioning church localities where twice a year—early spring and early fall—Sami gathered for a weekend of church activities. At these times an old Sami settlement would come alive again. It was one of the places where they'd built kota [hutlike structures built with wooden poles and covered with earth, often in the same shape as Sami skin-covered tents], to which people normally on the move would return from time to time.

It was here that I first made contact with Sami culture. I grew to have many Sami friends, including a boyfriend whom I would visit at his family's summer camp site about thirty-five miles from Ammarnäss. The Sami often mistook me for one of their own, due to my small size, the fact that I tan easily in the summer, and that I could move rapidly through the mountains. At our first meeting, my boyfriend's mother asked me if I was a Norwegian Sami. When he informed her than I was from Denmark she assumed that was a town in the Scanian provinces [in southwestern Sweden], which was the southernmost point in her map of the world. Since then I have been in Sami territory every year.

Very roughly, what has happened to the Sami culture in the thirty-some years that you have had personal contact with it?

Well, the most significant development has been the increasing sense of self-worth among the Sami, along with a growing pride in their own culture and the recognition that they must fight for the survival of their culture. This has, for example, resulted in demanding that the school system teach their children the Sami language. The problem here is that the Sami language only recently (in the past hundred years) has become a written language. Therefore, most of the cultural material hidden in the language remains untold, or known only to a few very old people.

Didn't the process of the destruction of the Sami culture start with the enforcement of Christianity approximately two hundred years ago?

I'm not in a position to evaluate that. I can only say that much of the Sami culture moved underground then and that it started to express itself in new ways, such as through myths. But horrendous things have been committed against the Sami culture. In Norway, for example, the Sami were forced to take Norwegian family names, which destroyed their knowledge of kinship relations, to mention only one among many devious means that have been employed to undermine Sami culture. They have naturally also been subject to the same economic forces as the rest of us and there is today a much greater gap between rich and poor Sami than ever before. In fact, a regular proletariat has evolved among the coastal Sami [in northwestern Norway], while in Sweden one can find quite well-to-do reindeer ranchers. Chernobyl has of course been devastating to many of these people. But it has affected the Sami differently depending on which country they live in, as each country has its own regulations concerning acceptable levels of radiation. So, the Swedish Sami were probably hit the hardest in economic terms. But it is impossible at this point to begin to estimate the devastation caused by Chernobyl.

There are about forty to fifty thousand Sami in Norway, fifteen to twenty thousand in Sweden, four to eight thousand in Finland, and maybe three thousand in the Soviet Union.

Are they allowed to move freely across borders?

Not at all to the extent they would like. There are some agreements between Norway, Sweden, and Finland, and there exists a pan-Scandinavian Sami Council. But the Sami on the Kola Peninsula are isolated. I was once involved in a committee under the Nordic Council which dealt with ways in which the Sami might participate in theater education in the Scandinavian countries. It was also at these meetings that the first formulations concerning Sami theater education were initiated. The Kola Sami were invited to participate but we never heard from them.

Do you have any sense of whether the Kola Sami have developed differently from other Sami, in cultural terms?

Yes, they have, but the Scandinavian Sami have also developed differently from one another depending on which country they lived in, and in accordance with the material conditions in which they found themselves.

How do the Sami relate to the four nation states in which they live?
They feel exploited. Their hunting and herding territories have been taken away through farming, and large hydro projects have destroyed grazing lands, and so forth. In some areas hunting rights have been sold to private interests; in others the right to fish salmon has been sold to foreign companies, who protect their property with armed guards. And in all these areas the reindeer are not allowed. However, the reindeer follow the wind, which still blows north, south, east, and west regardless of property rights. So, things have become quite difficult and complex. But the very big plans to destroy three or four towns through flooding, in order to build a large hydro dam by the Alta River in northern Norway, really activated the Sami in a huge protest where they had to fight the police. The Sami received massive support from Amerindian and Inuit environmental activists during this protest.

Why do you think that these kinds of assertions of rights are being expressed by the peoples of the Fourth World at this time?
It's happening now because they have observed quite clearly that the peoples of the so-called First World are in the process of poisoning themselves and the rest of the planet. The aboriginal peoples therefore feel culturally and materially threatened, and in order to defend themselves they begin to assert their uniqueness—the fact that they are not mixed, that they are original cultures. Not to mention the fact that there are very few of these cultures left on earth.

We need to question the notion of "aboriginality," though, don't we? These Fourth World cultures have also undergone incredible changes both within their own cultural histories as well as in response to "outside" contact. And they have often integrated with vigorous pleasure elements from the industrialized world, such as the snowmobile, a vehicle which is ruining much of northern ecology. In other words, I don't think that the background of an original culture carries with it some kind of moral purity or innocence.
I agree. The equation of moral innocence, and the desire for moral purity, with a natural and economic striving for independence can lead to some terrible conclusions, as history has shown. So, it is important to keep these two issues separate from one another.

In recent years, many of these cultures have taken to the use of theater, in the Western sense of the term, in order to express their self-worth to the rest of the world. They have begun to use a form of cultural expression not indigenous to their aboriginality. Could you talk about this as it relates to the Sami?

They have discovered that there exists a form of expression, of communication which others make use of in television, in touring theater productions, video, etc. And they wish to make use of these tools in expressing their own culture and their political and social agendas. My own role in this has simply been to teach dramaturgy that would have an effect through, for example, Swedish television. My function has been to teach them a tool whereby they could tell their own version of their history in a manner that could be understood by others. That process has been very simple, and then it's up to them if they want to use it—some do and some don't. The movie *The Pathfinder* [*Veiviseren,* written and directed by Nils Gaup] is a result of some of these efforts, a movie that certainly makes the most blatant use of Anglo-Saxon storytelling techniques. It is written completely according to [Syd Field's] formula, and it works extremely well as such, while it also leaves room for some moments of Sami *raisonnements* concerning their own situation and their sense of self-worth. What is left behind is nine-tenths of a storytelling tradition and a singing tradition which is almost totally lost but for a few old people who remember.

So, when I work with the Sami I see it as my function to stimulate the development of these memories, these traditions which can become the basis for many different kinds of theatrical expression. "You have so many different kinds of performance in your own culture. Develop those, and make as much use of the dramaturgy I'm telling you about as is useful to you. But let's make use of your own cultural tools. For example, let's take a look at how you move when you dance."

They move very differently from us. Their movements while dancing certainly don't inspire one to start working on a classical ballet. Their movements are naturally in tune with their environment and with their work habits. They are used to moving through the tundra with its small bushes and through deep snow. They do not move about stretching their necks in a swanlike fashion. That means that their traditions of movement are quite different from ours. It is, then, not my job at any time to outline what they should or should not do. My task is rather to assist them in an attempt to systematize the residual effects of their cultural expressions.

But their initial interest in making use of the theater lies in its usefulness as a propaganda tool.

Absolutely. Both in relationship to the outside world as well as internally, that is, both in order to communicate with the outside world and in order to preserve their culture.

You are, then, also assisting in a project of cultural archaeology.
I see it as a project of cultural archaeology. The part involving teaching them about Western storytelling techniques is rather simple. I am the one who is learning enormous amounts about life cycles and multiplicities and expressions of generous inclusion when I work with them.

How did this work get started?
The Nordic Theater Committee was approached by the Sami, who requested workshops in dramaturgy. There were at that time a few Sami professional actors who'd started theater groups. There are quite a few now. These groups arose to promote the Sami language, which in many areas is completely lost. Among others there was a small group from Hattfjelldal in Norway for whom I went to do a workshop. The average age in the group was seventy-three and there were only six of them who knew Southern Sami. So they were in a hurry to get started working. They came to this workshop in dramaturgy because they wanted to make children's theater, which they knew of through touring companies.

Are there any Sami playwrights?
There are a few who are in the process of becoming playwrights.

I am asking in an attempt to compare the Sami situation to that of the Inuit in Greenland, where a professional theater has existed in Nuuk since 1984, the Silamiut Theater. They tend to develop their shows through improvisation rather than working with playwrights.
The same holds true for a Sami theater group like Raugos, which is also about four years old.

Do you think there is a connection between Greenland's relatively recent achievement of home rule and the equally recent assertions of difference by other colonized cultures in the Nordic countries, such as the Sami and the Faeroe Islanders?
I think it fuels a hope as they witness the success of the Inuit in acquiring cultural independence. But I don't think that the Sami are modeling themselves on Greenland, although there are connections. When

the theater work began among the Sami, at least one of the professional actors was educated at the Tūkak' Theater. The Sami, and others, certainly see Tūkak' as the only real place of theater education for peoples of the Fourth World.

When did the first dramaturgical workshop you conducted take place?
That was in September 1985 in Kautokaino [Sami spelling: Guovda-geaidnu] in Norway. That was the first workshop in playwriting to which Sami writers were invited. This past spring [May 1988] we did a second one and we are planning a third one for the near future. In between, I am in constant correspondence with the Beaivvāš Theater in Kautokaino. Beaivvāš is the resident theatre in the cultural center up there, which also houses an institute for Sami research, as well as the Sami Council. I've also worked with the southern Sami in Hattfjelldal, where there's a very active group working to preserve the Sami language.

You've mentioned the issue of preserving the Sami language twice now. What are the real implications of the possible disappearance of a language?
A language doesn't actually die. It survives much, much longer than we now have any real sense of. It lives on in various forms. As an example I can mention the work of a wonderful Sami writer and academic, Agot Vinterbo-Hohr, who does not speak Sami but Norwegian, and in whose poetry a Sami consciousness and imagery is clearly evident—in almost every single poem she writes. In other words, one could say that images operating in the mind which are based in a different language are being translated into, in this case, Norwegian.

Through what kind of process is this possible?
I don't think it is a question of how this is possible, but rather whether it is possible not to do it. Is it then not possible to say that a language has disappeared because it still operates in the way we grammatically process into our new language images and relationships originating in the former language?

Are these resonances then part of a genetic inheritance?
Probably. You will see this evidence among quite a number of Sami writers who write in Norwegian but who use the language structurally

quite differently—Ailo Gaup is another example. But you can see the same process at work among French writers of Arabic extraction.

What does a regular workshop look like?

At the last workshop I conducted the writers were asked to bring material that they considered dramatic. They brought poems and scenarios. But no matter what it was we would discuss their intentions with the pieces. Then we discussed the specifics of how to translate these particular pieces into works for the stage. There was a natural disposition toward expressing things in non-Aristotelian ways and in visual terms, rather than in verbal terms. And the verbal expressions were frequently highly charged, lyrically speaking, in an almost musical fashion. The important thing for me in this process is always to facilitate their work, because I have no sense of one cultural expression and shaping being more valid than another. Multiplicity and change are key notions. One has to listen to the grass grow. But I also teach Aristotelian forms of story construction as a valuable tool.

How does one "hear the grass grow" in a workshop?

I listen for repetitions. I become sensitive to repetitions. There is an African proverb which states that when you start writing down your poems you've forgotten how to dance. I understand this statement deep in my soul. And when I am with the Sami, I listen and I watch—that is the beginning of the dramaturgical process. My questions to the writers often relate to other ways of expressing the same thing. "How would your grandparents express this?" Eventually a certain rhythm is uncovered, sometimes related to song, sometimes to dance. And when they begin to move they start to seek relationships on the stage from which the language then arises. And slowly we try to get back to the point just before they started to write. When the poet commits the poem to the page he/she has forgotten how to dance.

How do you produce the dance along with the poem?

Through the fundamental rhythm. It must be sought in a space. Brecht says somewhere that what he seeks is the *Gestus,* the gestural material in a situation. Listening for the grass growing in this manner among the Sami is unbelievably rewarding. They are a people of such tremendous variety, of acceptance, with a sense of multiplicity and the ability to absorb and encompass, as opposed to our stingy demarcations and need for control.

What's the next step in the workshop process?
I get them to move. Writers seem to have a peculiar relationship to their bodies. So, wherever in Scandinavia (or elsewhere) I conduct workshops for writers, movement becomes a very important warm-up exercise. I also require that the writers function as actors in one another's work. At the last workshop I did, all the actors and technicians of the theater participated, so we ended up with about thirty people. This was a true gift to the writers. So, I began mixing them in groups; theater is after all a joint effort. We were suddenly in an ideal situation. People began without my urging to exchange experiences. And we began to work practically with the materials that came out of that. We had very few theoretical discussions, because it's true you really do forget how to dance when you write down your poem.

Instead, we experimented with things like the stage picture, the visual elements, and so on. Quickly, we were moving toward political imagery, because they had specific things that they wanted to address: such as how the snowmobile was ruining the land, an issue which can only be addressed in Sami by the Sami—not by Swedish or Norwegian environmental activists. An issue like that belongs with other issues of Sami cultural affirmation. The discussion became very sharp and very specific, which was wonderful because I could then assume the attitude that "your struggle for liberation is completely irrelevant to me, whether you belong to the fourth, the seventeenth, or the twenty-first world is of no interest to me. These are the issues at hand and we have to relate to them here and now."

Do you see a relationship between cultural preservation and progressive social change?
Progressive social change is impossible without cultural preservation. But the important thing is to learn from the mistakes as well as the positive collective experiences of the past, not to build a museum for the preservation of culture.

So you see cultural archaeology as a radicalizing process?
Yes indeed. Because it initiates change and understanding, insight.

How do you avoid becoming a "controller" in this process?

I never assume that I know more than they do. I move toward "I know something different from them" and then toward "I know nothing." When I arrive at that point I'm able to teach, become a facilitator of knowledge. How they use this knowledge is their problem: in a certain sense I function amorally in the situation. Whether they want to produce propaganda or save their language, or whatever, remains completely their choice. In this way I can function within the love, inclusivity, and philosophical multiplicity which characterize the circumpolar peoples, opposed to operating as a controlling, authoritative, and therefore dangerous force. Their sense of the universe is much more holistic than ours.

Is there a connection between the growing interest among Western intellectuals in such matters as the increasing self-affirmation of the peoples of the Fourth World on one hand, and the scientific realization that our universe is ungoverned and characterized by chaos on the other?

Yes, I think recent scientific considerations have made us much more responsive to and accepting of difference and change. As the world seems to become smaller it is actually becoming a much larger place as we participate in it with greater variety and with expanded senses, so to speak.

How do we find the path(s) toward a situation which will allow us to preserve our different cultural "uniqueness" while at the same time develop (a) world culture(s) which is/are multiple, nonexclusive, and accepting?

Let me put it this way: As long as one needs a sense of power, of control, to suppress others and claim special status, needing to be seen as better than others via one's culture, then one simply isn't present in the world. One is then removed from one's own expression and from one's own culture. Power is then necessary to achieve self-affirmation. Whereas acceptance of multiplicity produces the opposite. I really believe that it comes down to not being afraid of the multiple, of simultaneity.

Where is the culture which doesn't assume that it's better than others? Isn't there an inherent conflict between the self-affirmed uniqueness of individual cultures and the notions of acceptance and multiplicity?

Yes, but let the individual cultures remain limited. We know that they are; we've seen through them, and we can begin to transcend those limitations. Affirmations of uniqueness can then move our thinking to a higher level.

What about the intracultural expressions of oppression? Don't the Sami, for example, within the culture they are in the process of regaining give expression to oppressive power relations?
Yes, but it is up to them to solve those issues. And they, like the rest of us, are under the influence of the greater insight which recent scientific thought makes possible.

My sense is that Sami culture is more cooperatively based than Western cultures are, generally speaking. How does this express itself in the way they produce theater?
They began by producing theater in the authoritative, hierarchical manner we do. But it didn't work for them, so they now work more collectively, though they have somebody named as heading the organization because the funding state ministries require that kind of administrative structure.

Why then educate specific playwrights for the Sami theater? It is one thing to develop a certain competence, another to encourage a specific division of labor.
I don't believe that one should. The case in point is the workshop that I mentioned earlier in which the actors and technicians of the theater participated and everything began to work much better. So, I think that they themselves are dissolving that kind of structure.

That way the Aristotelian dramaturgy, understood as the expression of a single individual's singular, linear story line (which is then directed and finally executed by some actors) becomes less prevalent.
Yes, they are widening the territory. I always teach that the Aristotelian is only one among many possible dramaturgies. I don't see any problem in that and I have no sense of aggression in connection with it. The drive for control is then replaced by insight and collective knowledge. I also believe that insight rather than control is fostered through intercultural work, through interculturalism.

The Trickster and Native Theater

An Interview with
Tomson Highway

William Morgan

Tomson Highway, Cree, is originally from northern Manitoba but has lived and worked in Toronto for many years. After eight years of working closely with Ontario's native community, he decided to involve himself in theater and in film. To this end he has written and produced several stage plays drawing on native myth as source and inspiration. His plays have received wide critical acclaim across Canada. He currently serves as artistic director of Native Earth Performing Arts, Inc., Toronto. The following is taken from a conversation with Tomson Highway on November 3, 1989, as well as from a public talk Mr. Highway gave that day.

You had a career as a concert pianist.
Well, it wasn't really a career.

At least you were preparing for one.
I was almost there, yes.

And you switched to theater. Why, may I ask, did you decide to do that?
Oh, I just didn't think that playing Chopin in concert halls had very much to do with Indian people. It was just so removed from where I come

from that I quit and went to work for Indian people, on the streets and in the bars.

So it was activism, if you will, that inspired your move.

Yes. I came into contact with Indian people on a very basic level, a very human level, very intimate. I just basically found out that their lives touched me deeply, and I just sort of started writing. I don't know why. I don't think it as really a rational decision. There is this black cloud, I think, that hangs over society at this point in history, particularly with respect to the environment, the ecology, you know, the ozone layer, oil spills, rain forests, etc., etc., and I think, we as a collective society, a universal human society, have come to a point in our history where things are going to have to change awfully drastically if we are going to have our own kids grow up to be any kind of human beings that have a respectable chance at a beautiful life on the planet. I really believe that going back to our spiritual roots, really, as far back as we possibly can, if we do that, we may come up with some possible answers to the dilemma that faces us at this point.

You chose a direction that had more heart for you then.

Yes. Now I can combine the best of the training I had—classical structure—because my musical instruction extended far beyond just playing piano, and into the basic structure of, for example, string quartets, sonatas, and opera, which brought me into the structure of Greek dramas, and the study of painting—Rembrandt, Fra Angelico. It was not just a matter of combining classical structure with Indian street reality and here we have these plays that, unlike classical forms, can speak to everyone.

I was interested to hear your comment [in a previous public talk] on the significance of the number seven in the structuring of some of your work. The Czechoslovakian novelist Milan Kundera writes of how his works each fall into seven parts. He as well had extensive training in classical music. Kundera says that the works of many classic composers contain a seven-part structure, and he believes that this is why, no matter how he starts out to write a novel, it will end up containing seven parts analogous to those musical compositions.

To tell the truth, this just seems to happen when I write, as it comes from my spine, my being.

That's just what Kundera says.
Is there something which we would want to call "native theater"?
Yes, I think it is now emerging and desperately trying to find its voice, and it will eventually, but right now it's still in its birth stage.

How would you see native theater as different from . . . non-native theater?
Well, the mythology. The use of underlying native mythology is the distinctive feature. Native mythology is so alive, electric, passionate, whereas I find in mainstream society, the relationship in Christian mythology is so academic by comparison. It has lost something, whether it's the Industrial Revolution that did it or not, I don't know, but we native people haven't historically had that break, and the contact is so visceral and I think that is the central feature, that is why native theater is attracting so much attention. That spiritual reality is there. It is magic.

It is then the spiritual dimension that gives it vitality. In non-native theater, you might have very powerful, activist social and political issues but they don't have that spiritual dimension that native theater has.
That's right, yes. I think Western-world art did have it at one time. I was in Florence just a while ago. You look at those paintings by Giotto and Fra Angelico. Western white man art, you know? It is passionately connected with God. It is amazing. Western art, at least here in Canada now, I don't sense that. Not that direct contact with the spiritual, that devotion. It needs to find it.

To move people.
Yes.

What do white people think of what you're doing? Is it interesting to them?
Sure. Fascinating. They didn't realize, first of all, that the mythology exists. It came as a total surprise to them. They are interested in it because it's colorful first of all, visually spectacular in theatrical presentations.

Do you think more non-native people are interested in native theater today than five or ten years ago?
Yes, but of course there was no native theater back then, also because

it has spiritual power for everyone. Many people are lacking in their own lives. There's a hunger there. Some people are pretty desperate.

Do you see a difference in the responses to your work in native and non-native audiences?
No. I think it's all the same. I like to write in such a way that it moves all people, moves rocks. Then, I guess my job has been done.

Then what you have to say through your plays is to people as human beings and not to people as native or non-native.
That's right. Ultimately.

Would not the significance of a number of things in your plays go by non-native people in an audience?
People have varying intellectual capabilities and some people are just more discerning than others regardless of whether they're native or non-native. There are smart white people and smart Indians, and stupid white people and stupid Indians. With respect to metaphor and symbols, as long as the basic plot line is there and solid, then as to what any audience member catches, that's their responsibility. The more they catch, the better. There's probably lots of stuff that nobody catches, but I put it down anyway. That gives it an additional layer of richness. Even the names of the characters have mythological resonance, usually within native mythology, but sometimes Greek myth. The Greek gods would come down to earth, mate with morals, and sire superheroes like Hercules. There is a direct link between humans and the spirit world as in native myth. This gives an added layer of resonance, of richness; if nobody catches this in lines of my plays, that's okay. It seems that most white people I meet don't know anything much about Greek mythology, to my amazement. And yet, that is part of their cultural and spiritual roots. I know it and I'm not white.

The Trickster, Wasageechak or Nanabush, is a central figure in your plays to date.
To date.

Obviously this is a figure with tremendous relevance for you in speaking to native and non-native audiences, to society at large.
Yes, for my people, that figure was almost killed. If he/she (there is

not a male/female distinction to be made here; Cree doesn't work like that) had been killed, we would not exist today. I am basically pissed off at what happened when the two cultures came in to contact with each other. This clown, this good-time guy, was told that he had no business laughing and having a good time. That's bullshit. We're going to bring him back regardless. It's an obsession at this point in life. Maybe it's not for everybody, but it's my life. I mean I could talk about Sioux mythology, Ojibway, etc., but Cree is the one I know best. We have these stories about why??—what the hell we are doing here on the face of the earth and why do we bother going on with life tomorrow and tomorrow and tomorrow—and this dream world of Cree mythology is peopled, it is inhabited by the most fantastic creatures and beings and events. Central of which is this incredible creation, this extraordinary figure of the imagination called the Trickster. Weesakayjuc, we call him in Cree. The Ojibway people call him Nanabush. People of the West Coast call him Herraven, Coyote down in the States, etc., etc. I suppose that is the closest kind of central hero figure we have, usually that is a half-man, half-god figure that makes that central connecting link to the Great Spirit. Just as within the realm of Christian mythology you likewise have this half-man, half-god hero figure who makes the central connection of your Great Spirit, this gentleman by the name of Jesus Christ, we have this clown. Ours is a clown, ours is a laughter, ours is a good-time guy and basically one super-hero. . . . I was inundated with Roman Catholic education at a boarding school in The Pas, Manitoba, for nine years. I went to high school here in Winnipeg as well, but I can't help trying to figure out my life, and the way I think and the way my mind works help to make comparisons between these two mythologies, not exactly similar by any stretch of the imagination.

I suppose you are touching the tip of an enormous iceberg when you start going into this kind of heavy subject matter, but I would like to encapsulate it for you very briefly by pointing out a couple, at least three or four telling differences to give you a comparative idea of these two mythologies. Basically, one superhero is stating that we are here to suffer and the other basically says we are here to have one helluva good time. One was crucified, the other wasn't; so we have absolutely nothing to feel guilty about. This, because the other telling thing that comes into the picture is the very element of linguistic structure. In the English, Italian, French, German, and other European languages you can't help but make comparisons between the distinct linguistic histories and traditions. The most amazing thing that I find about the European languages that differs from us is that in Cree there is no gender, whereas in the European languages you always have to deal with the male/female/neuter hierarchy. The Cree and the other native languages are structured in such a way that we look at the universe not according to that hierarchy but according to a dichotomy consisting of that in the universe which is animate, which has a living, breathing spirit, and that which is inanimate, which has no living, breathing spirit, so that by that system, a human being, a man, a woman, a tiger, a tree, even a rock are all structured in such a way that you would address a tree on the same level as you would address a man or a woman or a cat. Contrariwise, if you cut that tree down and you take that piece of wood, this piece of wood for instance, this has no living, breathing animate spirit and therefore this is inanimate, and only then do you refer to it as "it."

So, whereas—going back to comparing the Christian and the Cree mythologies—whereas one superhero figure is definitely a male, definitely a man, in our mythology by virtue of the fact that the sexual hierarchy is completely absent, theoretically, our superhero figure is neither exclusively male nor exclusively female or is both, simultaneously interchangeable. And so those are some of the key differences in the two mythologies in the way they work.

And the Trickster—this is an English term of course—tricks people into what?

Well, he tries to trick people, but more often than not the tricks backfire on him, and he gets caught in his own doings. All the stories are like that. Inadvertently, he gets caught up in these ridiculous, sometimes quite horrifying situations. He tries to find his way out using his intellect, but it never works, and it's only inadvertently, through some other visceral, emotional, irrational part of him/her, that a way is found out of the situation only to teach us, in the end, a telling lesson about life. In my plays you find characters who are a modernization of the essential elements of the classic Trickster.

So Wasageechak does not set up clever tricks to trick people into seeing things as they really are in spite of their former illusions about how things work. The Trickster figure you employ is rather a bit of a klutz in some ways.

Yes. The Trickster in the myths I draw from embodies aspects of both good and evil. Whereas in the Christian structure there is God, who takes all the glory for himself and blames all the evil on Satan, and some go to Heaven and some to Hell. Yet we as human beings are as equally capable of evil as of good.

The Trickster as you use the figure partakes more of human characteristics, including negative ones, than spiritual figures in Christianity do.
Christ, of course, is human and divine.

But he doesn't make the errors, blunders that Wasageechak does.
The Trickster is more like us in those ways, yes.

Moving back to Native Earth Performing Arts, where would you like to see it go? What might it accomplish?
I would like to see it establish a body of native dramatic literature that is really powerful and beautiful . . . like what the Abbey Theatre did in Dublin. I think it has that kind of capability with a tremendous amount of hard work. It can establish the voice of native people. With the existence of top-notch scripts comes the acting skill. I think the quality of those scripts will challenge native actors. The scripts will come first in time.

Some of the actors in your plays are not native, is that not correct?
Sure, we used a white actor in our last show. But he plays a white man, you know.

It's okay, I'm not looking for a part. Could a non-Algonkian native actor play a part you have written for a Cree, or Ojibway, or Saulteaux and play it to your satisfaction, do you think?
With hard work, love, and dedication it is possible, I believe. With integrity. I subscribe to nontraditional casting. I think a black actor is capable of playing Hedda Gabler, or a Cree Indian and vise versa.

When we think of Algonkian people, in the past as in the present, we think of individuals and communities performing rituals and ceremonies on a frequent basis. How do you see theater as different from that and does it take up some of those functions that ritual and ceremony has for native people? Does the stage presentation of a play by a native playwright, with native mythological themes and actors, do for native people

*in the audience some of the things that ritual and ceremony would have
done in earlier, more traditional times in a community context?*

I believe so. In Europe theater had its start in the context of religious
ritual. Theater at its most effective and pure form is like a church. And
in *Dry Lips*, there are moments when it's almost like that.

*Would the quality of the experience or action presented in your plays
be anything like an experience of ritual, say, in a northern reserve
situation?*

Well, they're not literally depicted but there are some twists of plot,
some situations which are very like ceremonies.

*In the Christian tradition when you enter a church and there is ritual
and there is ceremony you are being presented with the way things "are."
You are to believe that you are coming into contact with the actual forces
governing the universe. In the cultural mainstream, however, when you
go to see a play there is the characteristic expectation of the observer's
"willing suspension of disbelief." You are looking at something that is
consciously fictional and you are not expected to believe that "reality" is
going on there, as you are in the case of the church-based performance.
Is there that kind of difference between traditional native ritual and
ceremony on the one hand, and what is happening onstage in your plays,
or are both "reality" situations? Am I being at all clear?*

I don't know [long pause]. Yes, I'll try my best to respond. In my
plays some things that happen are pretty realistic and there are some things
that happen that are pretty unrealistic and magical and otherworldly, but
the human imagination is capable of handling both. In the performance
of ritual in the Roman Catholic Church, there are elements of hard-core
physical reality and also elements that are in a sense, if you want to call
it that, like a fiction. Drinking the blood of Christ, you know, when you
come right down to it you're actually drinking a glass of wine. When
you're eating a host, a piece of unleavened bread, that's the Body of
Christ. Some uninformed, exaggerated objective opinion on that might
ask if that is advocating cannibalism. So the wine and the host are not
just symbolic acts, they are consecrated acts. There is an aspect of "this
is real" about them. The next writer that we have [coming up on the
program], in "Diary of a Crazy Boy," comes up with some pretty interesting questions along those lines. He brings into the picture the native
figures of the Little People, mythical characters something like elves, and

a four-hundred-year-old spirit that comes to guide a native boy. A white doctor asks: "Why do you believe in that stuff?" And the young boy says: "Why do you believe in angels, the Host, the wine, and all that stuff?" I do think all mythologies are equally viable. Some of the differences and similarities, I don't understand yet.

I think we are all working on these things in our own ways.
Yes.

Recovering a Language

An Interview with Knut Walle
and Kurt Hermansen of the
Beaivváš Theater

Per Brask

Knut Walle (b. 1949 at Vesterålen) and Kurt Hermansen (b. 1948 at Oksfjord) were both instrumental in the creation of the Beaivváš Sami Theater in the early 1980s. Knut Walle trained as an actor at the State Theater School and Kurt Hermansen took a variety of theater courses in Norway and Denmark, after which he specialized in lighting design. They are presently the artistic director and the producer, respectively, of the Beaivváš. The following was taken from a conversation in Tromsø, Norway, on August 11, 1990—the day after the opening of a new show based on the long poem *The Courtship of the Son of The Sun in the Land of the Giants,* by the Sami poet Anders Fjellner (1795–1876).

The conversation took place in Norwegian and Danish and was translated by the interviewer.

Tell me about the origins of the Beaivváš.

KNUT WALLE: Ailo Gaup, the poet, had written a series of poems which dealt with the exploitation of nature, specifically by the Norwegians. Which at the time, 1980, was extremely relevant because the expansion of a hydro dam between Alta and Guovdageaidnu met with a lot of resistance. This resistance eventually led to confrontations with the police. People lay down in linked rows in front of the construction machinery, and there were hunger strikes in front of the parliament in

Knut Walle, artistic director
(1980–90), the Beaivváš
Theater, Guovdageaidnu,
Norway. Photograph by Per
Brask.

Kurt Hermansen, producer
(1980–90), the Beaivváš
Theater, Guovdageaidnu,
Norway. Photograph by Per
Brask.

Oslo. In Guovdageaidnu there was a group of young people involved in the music scene who wanted to develop a rock musical around these events. They got a number of people involved who worked in the established professional theater. For example Kurt, who worked at Nationaltheatret in Oslo, as a lighting designer. And I who was working there as an actor. We were in contact with the Sami actor Nils Gaup, who was working at Trøndelag theater. Nils knew the people in Guovdageaidnu and that was how we got involved in creating the musical. So I began working with those thirty-five or so poems by Ailo Gaup and out of that we fashioned a fairly classically structured musical on the American model with a story, time for a song, the story continues, and so on. Like the poems we called the show *Våre vidder* [Our Mountains] and it dealt with the exploitations of nature while telling a story about youth and love, describing how a young enthusiastic Norwegian woman falls in love with the exotic Sami, leading to an inter-ethnic love affair where everything ends happily. Even the police are fought back and the mine (our literary transposition from the actual hydro dam) which was at stake in the play, doesn't get built. We wrote the show while the struggles at Alta were taking place and we prepared it to take part in the fight to stop the hydro project. That was the beginning of Beaivváš.

Who produced this show?

KNUT WALLE: I directed it, Nils Gaup created the choreography, and we produced it independently by being able to raise funds from many different sources. We toured the show throughout Scandinavia. The show inspired a great deal of enthusiasm and an excitement about creating a permanent Sami theater.

What does Beaivváš mean?

KURT HERMANSEN: (It means both "the little sun" and "the little day."

How did you experience the difference between working in the established Norwegian theater and now working in a theater drawing on the Sami background?

KNUT WALLE: For me it was quite a change as I am not of Sami background.

KURT HERMANSEN: I am Sami, but I was educated in the Norwegian theater. So, for me it meant a great personal change.

Many of the theater groups who are dedicated to giving voice to aboriginal minorities have, at times, in the process of their development been led by non-natives or had non-natives in significant positions of leadership. Have you any thoughts about how that process works?

KNUT WALLE: This is quite a sensitive and problematic subject. The fact that the leadership of some of these groups has come from the outside reflects on the one hand the reality that in many of those groups the theatrical expertise has not existed. On the other hand, this produces a great many conflicts that arise naturally out of making theater, which requires living in a new way with new forms of discipline and an ability to work collectively. Sometimes, these conflicts are attributed to cultural and ethnic differences rather than to the necessity of maintaining a working climate that is conducive to producing theater. I think that it's a pity that the Sami who in fact are educated in the theater haven't involved themselves more actively in the leadership of Sami theater instead of seeking employment in the established Norwegian theater. Because if they did many of those kinds of conflicts would be much easier to manage.

Is it a form of cultural imperialism to develop theater groups in cultures for whom the theater (in the standard Western sense of the term) is indeed foreign?

KNUT WALLE: No, I definitely do not think that it is cultural imperialism to start theater groups in other cultures! We're talking about an exchange between people. It is one of the ways that a minority group can show its strength. In addition, the expressed desire to make theater is not enough to make it happen; it requires a certain expertise, and if you despise the expertise developed in Western theater, then get it from somewhere else. Expertise, however, is essential. The Sami theater has indeed drawn a great deal on Western theater traditions, and recently with a little funding and with glasnost it has become possible to draw on even more backgrounds. But when taking about the establishment of new theaters it is important to be realistic about their development.

In the show you opened last night it is evident that you have drawn on many different forms of movement and dance, traditional as well as contemporary, in order to create a unique hybrid performance style which depends heavily on theatrical images. Many contemporary aboriginal groups seem to develop forms that are heavily imagistic in expression. Is this because many of these groups work both to recover languages that have been disappearing and very often also perform to non-natives?

KURT HERMANSEN: Yes, I think that's so. For Beaivváš the language is very important. The language as well as the culture must be brought to the next generation. And, of course, our theater works in a very visual style, making use of all the tools of the theater. And for this combination we've received extremely good response. Our last show was Lorca's *Blood Wedding,* which is very much based in language, and in that case we were very well received by our Sami audiences while other audiences were less enthusiastic.

During The Courtship of the Son in the Land of the Giants, *which otherwise opened to a standing ovation last night, a few Sami could be seen leaving during the performance. When I later inquired as to the reason I was informed that some Sami were upset at the use of electronic music and the overt sexuality displayed in your interpretation of Fjellner's poem.*

KNUT WALLE: Well, there are those who believe that electronic music is not for the Sami. However, I happen to believe that this is an available form of expression which is there for the use of the Sami as well as for anyone else. And, I have not acted imperialistically and insisted on the use of electronic music. That I left for the Sami composers to decide. The sexuality of the show comes from the clear sexual undertones running all the way through the poem we used as our text. But there will among any people, naturally, be differences of opinion as to what is appropriate and what isn't. Ethnophobic attitudes, however, are dangerous for any culture. Sami culture has often been suppressed through silence and it is time to come forward. The joik [traditional Sami song] is not the only important way for Sami to perform. We can do many more things than that.

The play Gesat *focuses specifically on the subject of identity. How did you, Knut, and Nils Gaup arrive at this play?*

Well, Nils Gaup and I found ourselves in the position of working as actors here in Tromsø. We were frustrated over the kinds of roles that were available and we decided that we had to create something for ourselves. Nils knew about those two great Sami artists, Aikio and Savio, and brought up the idea of doing a fictional meeting between the two of them. Some academics had done a great deal of work about the two of them; we got hold of it and we started to work on it. Sverre Porsanger joined us. He and Nils played the two artists and I directed it. The issues of identity and how one uses oneself as an artist were very much at the forefront of our concerns then, as the experiences from the struggle against the hydro dam where still fairly recent—a struggle which we had lost. The positive effect of this defeat was that the fight itself had made people consider their Sami heritage. People began to form associations and to reconstruct forgotten customs of dress from old photos. The whole issue of being of Sami background, which earlier had been more or less a taboo subject, took on a different character. So, when we worked on *Gesat* we wanted to look at these issues.

How were you affected, Kurt, as a Sami, by these changed cultural circumstances taking place in the early 80s?

KURT HERMANSEN: I had until then always had problems with being a Sami. In fact, I had learned to suppress my Sami background. If I found myself in a situation where I had to give an answer I would usually say that I had some Finnish blood in me. So when I started to work with Sami theater in 1981 it became something huge and fantastic to be in a place where I could be proud of being Sami. My life was revolutionized. It was a very strange and wonderful experience. And now, as I'm finishing off at the Beaivváš, I'm looking forward to going back into the Norwegian theater and telling them of my experiences.

Yesterday I met a Sami in his mid-60s who was unhappy that he had never learned the Sami language. His father had been a teacher and because he was very obedient he carried out the prohibition against teaching the Sami language in his home as well.

KURT HERMANSEN: I have never owned the Sami language. I heard the language from my grandparents but after them it disappeared. That's the situation for a great many Sami. The new generation of Sami will be better off now that there's been an amendment to the Norwegian constitution making Sami and Norwegian equal languages.

How do non-Sami-speaking Sami react to your performances when you are on tour?

KURT WALLE: The reaction is usually very warm, mixed, a resigned sadness that they don't understand the whole show. But we have never heard negative reactions to the fact that we perform in Sami. And, I think that it is of the utmost importance that we do. Our shows become a way of beginning to learn a little Sami, even if only to be able to say "hello." Not to mention that there are many small villages spread all over where Sami is spoken, and the people there have a right to see their language used.

Is it this circumstance of language which has pushed you toward a very visual form of communication in your theater?

KNUT WALLE: I think so. I mean, after all, we don't want to be rejected because of the language.

KURT HERMANSEN: I think it's important for us to perform in the Sami language. Dalvadis in Sweden has received a great deal of criticism for performing as much as they do in Swedish and in English. We want to keep the language active.

In your shows there are people from various backgrounds, Sami, Norwegian, Inuit. Is it part of your policy to engage in what in North America is termed nontraditional casting?

KNUT WALLE: No, that's just the way it's turned out. Our policy is actually that the company would consist of Sami-speaking actors, not just

Sami actors but Sami-speaking. But we're in a situation where a number of the younger actors are attending the Sami theater school in Finland and until they are educated we will have to wait. We see it as one of our functions to give jobs to Sami-speaking actors. At the same time, however, it is always important to bring people in from all over the world.

Now that you are both about to leave the Beaivváš, what does the future hold for the company?

KNUT WALLE: I think the future looks bright for Beaivváš. Even though the Norwegian state is a little slow to give us the money we need. But artistically, things are looking very promising.

KURT HERMANSEN: We currently have a budget of Nkr 5.3 million [approx. $850,000] and the smallest Norwegian-speaking regional theater located in Førde has a budget of Nkr 9.0 million [approx. $1.4 million], which in both instances is covered by the state. We, however, serve a district that is ten to fifteen times larger than theirs.

KNUT WALLE It is expensive to run a theater properly. In our company everyone is paid according to union rules, so something like 80 to 85 percent of our budget is spent on salaries and on touring.

KURT HERMANSEN: We have ten full-time staff, of which four are actors and the rest work with administration, technical areas, and artistic direction. We don't pay rent on our premises in Guovdageaidnu.

A few years ago the world become familiar with Sami drama through the film The Path Finder. *Was this film an outgrowth of the work of Beaivváš?*

KNUT WALLE: No, it came about because of the work of Nils Gaup. But perhaps one could ask whether such a film would ever have been possible without the existence of Beaivváš. Clearly the film sprang from Nils's imagination, but the circumstances that made it possible to make the film with Sami actors, for example, would have been different if Beaivváš had not been established seven years earlier.

Designed by Glen Burris
Set in Times Roman and Frutiger by WorldComp
Printed on 50 lb. M-V Eggshell Cream by
The Maple Press Company

PN 2219.3 .A26 1992

Aboriginal voices

DATE DUE			